The Age of Digital Marketing:
Master the Power of Facebook Advertising for Insanely Effective Social Media Marketing

Matthew Bartnik

CONTENTS:

Introduction	7
Facebook Usage Statistics	8
Usage Statistics	9
Marketing Statistics	9
Self-Serve Facebook Advertising	11
Chapter 1: Facebook Advertising versus Google AdWords	14
A Massive Audience	16
A Level Playing Field	17
A Variety of Ad Formats to Choose	17
The Advantages and Strengths of Facebook Ads	18
Unmatched Audience Granularity	18
A Visual Platform	19
Incredible ROI	20
Google Ad Words vs Facebook Ads: Where to Invest?	20
Facebook vs AdWords: What's Right for Your Business?	21
B2B Marketing	21
Retargeting	22
Facebook vs AdWords	23
B2C Marketing	23
Where Facebook May Not Be the Best Option	23
Allow Data to Decide	24
Chapter 2: Defining your Advertising Goals and Objectives	25
How to measure the efficacy of your campaigns:	26
What Tools do you use to Calculate the ROI of Your Campaigns?	
	27

How do we Conduct A/B tests to Measure Effectiveness of
Campaigns? 28
Simple Steps for Effective Online Marketing Strategies 32

Chapter 3: Finding & Evaluating Your Niche & Your Audience — 34

Finding Specific Niches Using Facebook Advertising 35
Evaluating the Profitability of Your Audience 39
Tools to Use to Evaluate the Profitability of Your Niches 43
Conclusion 46

Chapter 4: Paid Ads vs. Creating Free Content on Facebook — 47

Facebook Ads vs. Boosted Posts: Which Should You Choose? 47
When to use the full Facebook Ads vs Boosted Posts? 50
Pros and Cons of Creating Paid Ads vs. Creating Free Content to
Encourage More Organic Growth and Traffic 51

Chapter 5: Building a Company Facebook Page — 56

How to open a Facebook Page? 56

Chapter 6: Biggest Mistakes People Make with Facebook Ads — 61

1. Targeting Mistakes 61
2. Low Audience and Offer Match 62
3. Targeting Audiences That Are Too Broad 64
4. Not Leveraging Custom Audiences 65
5. Not Excluding Past Converters 65
6. Using the Wrong Ad Type 66
7. Ads That Fail to Draw Attention 67
8. Too Much Text on the Ad Image 68
9. Headlines without the Right Hook 68
10. Careless Copywriting 69
11. Missing a Clear Value Offer 70

12. Stuffing Ads with Too Much Text	71
13. Forgetting to Caption Video Ads	71
14. Bad Choice of Ad Placement	72
15. The 24/7 Ad Delivery	73
16. Amateur Ad Bidding	74
17. Slow Campaign Take-Off	75
18. Leaving Facebook No Time for Optimization	75
19. Guessing, Not Testing	76
20. Doing the Wrong Kind of A/B Tests	76
21. Testing Too Many Things at Once	77
22. Low Landing Page and Facebook Ad Match	77
23. Poor Landing Page UX	78
24. Neglecting the Conversion Tracking	78
25. Losing Sight of the Real Goal	79
26. Leaving Ads Unattended	80
27. Neglecting the Ad Frequency	80
28. Not Using Auto-Optimization	81
29. Missing Out on the Conclusions	83
Chapter 7: Understanding Facebook Advertising	84
Link Click Ads	89
Video Ads	90
Boosted Page Posts	90
Multi-Product (Carousel Ads)	91
Dynamic Product Ads (DPA)	92
Facebook Lead Ads	92
Canvas Ads	94
Collection Ads	94

Like & Engagement for Your Page	95
Page Like Ads	95
Page Post Photo Ads	96
Page Post Video Ads	96
Page Post Text	97
Mobile and Desktop Apps Install	97
Mobile App	98
Desktop App	98
Instagram Mobile App Ads	99
Event Ads	100
Local Awareness Ads	101
Who are your customers?	102
How to Create Facebook Audiences	102
Facebook Custom Audiences	105
How to Narrow Down Your Audiences	108
Facebook Ads Reporting & Optimization	108
Chapter 8: Psychology of Facebook Ads	113
Conclusion	118

© Copyright 2018 by Matthew Bartnik All rights reserved. The following eBook is reproduced below with the goal of providing information that is as accurate and reliable as possible. Regardless, purchasing this eBook can be seen as consent to the fact that both the publisher and the author of this book are in no way experts on the topics discussed within and that any recommendations or suggestions that are made herein are for entertainment purposes only. Professionals should be consulted as needed prior to undertaking any of the action endorsed herein. This declaration is deemed fair and valid by both the American Bar Association and the Committee of Publishers Association and is legally binding throughout the United States.

Furthermore, the transmission, duplication, or reproduction of any of the following work including specific information will be considered an illegal act irrespective of if it is done electronically or in print. This extends to creating a secondary or tertiary copy of the work or a recorded copy and is only allowed with an expressed written consent from the Publisher. All additional rights reserved. The information in the following pages is broadly considered to be a truthful and accurate account of facts and as such any inattention, use, or misuse of the information in question by the reader will render any resulting actions solely under their purview. There are no scenarios in which the publisher or the original author of this work can be in any fashion deemed liable for any hardship or damages that may befall them after undertaking information described herein.

Additionally, the information in the following pages is intended only for informational purposes and should thus be thought of as universal. As befitting its nature, it is presented without assurance regarding its prolonged validity or interim quality. Trademarks that are mentioned are done without written consent and can in no way be considered an endorsement from the trademark holder.

Introduction

We have all come in contact with Facebook Ads, whether we realize it or not. In this book, we will discuss the important facets of Facebook Advertising from what it is, whether it is important for your business, the how-to's, and many other great incentives that advertisers and marketers need to know.

It's 2018 and by now, you know that everywhere you look on the internet, you will be bombarded with ads. Facebook data is one of the most important ways 3rd parties collect information about consumers to effectively market to them. Facebook heavily influences people's online habits and Facebook ads, when used effectively, can be some of the most powerful tools to a digital marketer. So, what are they? We see them all the time, but do we know anything about them?

Here's a little info about Facebook Ads:
1. With Facebook ads, you are generally in control of your creative elements as you are the advertiser. This includes the title of the ad, the images used, the design, and the text.
2. Facebook ads use an auction type method wherein those who want to use Facebook ads are charged based on the clicks they receive, the impressions the ad gets, and the actions they results in. There are different formats of ads that Facebook offers which users can use.
3. You can craft and create all the different types of ads on your own or use Facebook's interface which enables you to self-service. If you need to work on your ads using a more wide-ranging tool, you can use certified API ad developers such as Qwaya.

4. Facebook ads can be categorized according to: i) Ads, and ii) Sponsored stories. Here are the different types of ads that you can create with Facebook ads. There are 10 kinds in total:

- Mobile App Ad
- Event Ad.
- Page post photo Ad
- Page Post Text Ad
- Domain Ad
- App Ad
- Page Like Ad
- Offer Ad
- Page Post Ads
- Page Post Link Ad
- Page Post video Ad

The places these ads will appear depends on the type you choose to use.

Facebook Usage Statistics

Believe it or not, not every business is on Facebook simply because they feel it is important to be interacting and engaging with their customers or target market on other social media channels like Twitter, Instagram, YouTube, and LinkedIn, and that may work fine for them. On the other hand, if you are planning to reach a wider audience, you might want to rethink and focus your marketing efforts to include Facebook as well. Here are some stats to enlighten you on the power of Facebook:

Usage Statistics

- Active users. On June 30, 2017, Facebook reached a total of 2.09 billion active, monthly users.

- There is an average of 79% of Americans use Facebook.

- There are 50 million businesses using Facebook Pages.

- A total of 22% of the world's population uses Facebook.

- Every minute, there are at least 400 new users signing up for a Facebook Account.

- There are at least 1.2 billion monthly active users engaging and communicating via Facebook Messenger.

- At least 83% of parents with children aged 13 to 17 years old are friends with their child on Facebook.

- Facebook is currently available in 101 languages.

Marketing Statistics

- 1 pm and 3 pm on Thursdays and Fridays are the most active times of usage for Facebook.

- Facebook Page content reach an average of 2.6 percent of organic reach.

- Pages that have smaller followings have a higher reach and higher engagement rates.

- Facebook is currently ranked as the most important platform for marketers.

- On average, brands post 8 times each day.

- 57% of consumers say that Facebook has influenced their shopping.

- User-generated content has more traction compared to brand-generated content, often creating a 6.9 times engagement rate.

- Finance and the Insurance industries have the highest cost-per-click on Facebook at $3.77.

- The apparel industry has the lowest cost per click at $0.45

- 93 percent of advertisers use Facebook ads.

- 4 to 15 words for a link description is the most effective length for ad titles on Facebook.

- Images make up to 75 percent to 90 percent performance for Facebook ads.

- $9.16 billion is Facebook's advertising revenue for 2017.

- 26% of Facebook users reported that they made a purchase after clicking on ads.

Facebook Marketing

Plenty of industry insiders who use Facebook understand its monetization models. However, not many understand how Facebook actually makes money.

Facebook has various revenue streams which include both past and future revenues.

The single most important revenue channel on Facebook is advertising. Facebook, at its core, has always been supported by ads since Facebook ad revenue regeneration is about half a billion each year. So, who pays for the advertising?

Self-Serve Facebook Advertising

Facebook's self-serve ad platform is where it gets its largest advertising revenue. You can literally start your own ad campaign on Facebook by following its step-by-step guide. These ads are located at the sidebar on most pages on Facebook cover events, user profiles, groups, as well as third-party apps. Granular targeting is the primary advantage of this platform.

Over the past few years, Facebook has tried to make their advertising more targeted by offering things like limiting your ad to metropolitan areas, zeroing in on variable targets such as age, gender, workplace, school, relationship status, and specific keywords.

Facebook has also released its Facebook Ads API. This gives large buyers and managers the capacity to build comprehensively on top of their existing advertising platform.

This Facebook Ads API will mostly help advertisers who spend a large amount of money a day just for modifying existing ads and posting new ones. Currently, the largest purchaser of Facebook's self-serve ads is Zynga who is also the developer of the largest games on Facebook such as Cafe World and Farmville. Of course, there are other advertisers who contribute to Facebook's revenue such as restaurants, societies, pet shops, lawyers, and doctors.

Engagement Ads

A substantial percentage of income for Facebook is from Engagement Ads. These types of ads can be placed on the homepage of the website which is an ideal solution especially for big brand names.

Users who enter the website would be able to interact with these ads. These ads are commonly found in the brand's homepage on the right-hand side. Facebook is always striving to create more avenues to attract brand advertisers and marketers, and with the launch of Brand Lift, Facebook is definitely taking the ad game to a whole new level. With Brand Lift, advertisers can test huge campaigns and study and scale their effectiveness. Brand Lift is also designed to maximize the level of measurement. This will hopefully encourage the brand advertisers to shell out more money on Facebook Engagement Ads.

Virtual Goods and the Marketplace

Facebook also makes a large amount of revenue from its Market Place or even its Gift Shop feature. Through Gift Shop or Marketplace, users can buy and sell products to one another. Facebook Marketplace has generated almost $100 million in revenue which makes it a very lucrative business.

The Marketplace has become a place to even purchase gifts for victims of a tragedy. In 2108, Facebook can expect to generate about $180 million just from the Marketplace alone.

Facebook Credits

Facebook Credits Stream is another way where Facebook can generate revenue. This used to be the way Facebook users could purchase virtual goods through Facebooks Gift Shop, but since Facebook has opened up this option to third-party developers, Facebook credits cannot be directly added into applications such as Farmville.

Facebook is greatly expected to continue expanding its platform to offer marketers more and more ways to advertise. This expansion also means that brands can look toward growing revenue by leaps and bounds.

Section 1 Conclusion:
- Advertising still remains the revenue channel of Facebook despite it making revenues from other sources.
- Self-serve ads are still the number one choice of ads for any booming business. Facebook has been experiencing continued growth and is showing no signs of stopping any time soon. As long as advertising is bringing in the big bucks for Facebook, it is unlikely that Facebook will start charging brands to open Facebook pages.

Chapter 1: Facebook Advertising versus Google AdWords

Many advertisers and marketers kept viewing Facebook Ads and Google AdWords in an adversarial way. It was thought that these two long-standing rivals were in direct competition with one another. Marketers were trying to see which one was best as if it was only necessary to choose one for their needs.

This is a false idea that until today is confusing and misleading in the online advertising avenue.

While you may think that these two big and brilliant brands are seen as competitors, the truth is, both of these brands co-exist. They serve different functions and many brands benefit from both Google AND Facebook Ads. What you should be doing when you want to achieve increased leads, maximum visibility, attract new customers, and acquire more sales is to leverage from the strengths of both Facebook Ads and Google.

For marketers and advertisers, you need to come up with different strategies that work on the strengths of each platform because this will bring in exceptional returns on your marketing expenditures. In this chapter, we will look into both of these types of advertising, the pros, and cons of each as well as which one you should consider using in your strategy on digital marketing.

Google Ad Words and Facebook Ads–The Difference

Before deciding anything, you need to familiarize yourself with the features of both these advertising platforms and also understand the fundamental differences between the two.

Google Ad Words: Paid Search

Currently, Google AdWords is the most popular of PPC (Pay-Per-Click) advertising. In the online advertising world, AdWords is what it is usually referred to as (and is so synonymous with) paid search. In paid search, the text-based advertisements as well as the specific keywords are used to describe a brand or a product.

Advertisers use AdWords to bid on keywords that are unique to their brand and that are commonly used by Facebook users to search brands, products, or services. By bidding on these keywords, marketers, and advertisers hope that their ads or business will come upon the user's search results.

The advertisers will get a certain amount of money when an ad is clicked by a user. This is what it means by "pay-per-click advertising."

Bid optimization and PPC bidding is a complex element in itself which you need to thoroughly learn in order to use. In its very essence, advertisers pay for the probability of finding new customers via keywords and phrases that they think users will potentially use when they look for things on Google.

Facebook Ads: Paid Social

Facebook ads can be categorized as "paid social" and they are one of the most prime examples relevant to today's online advertising world. Facebook has the distinction of having the highest quantity of MAUs or monthly active users and it is a profitable element of today's digital advertising repertoires.

While you can say that Facebook ads work similarly to the way Google Adwords works, the fundamentals are different and advertisers use both platforms to promote themselves on digital avenues. And this is where the similarity stops.

A business can use paid search to acquire fresh users utilizing the specific keywords. Users find businesses in paid social based on the things they are interested in or like.

The common difference between Facebook Ads and AdWords are:
Now that we have looked into the main composites of Facebook Ads and Google AdWords or in other words paid social and paid search, let's look into the strengths for each of these platforms and how these different tools can be used to your advantage.

The Benefits of Google AdWords

Google is the existing leader in online advertising, procuring the name of the most used and most popular search engine. Google amasses a total of 3.5 billion searches every single day. For marketers, Google is a gold mine that has an unequal and unprecedented pool of users who are always in search of goods and services to fulfill their needs and pain points.

They are divided into two main channels:
1. **The Search Network:** The search network is what Google is all about. Google is first and foremost a search engine and all its products are built around that fact. Advertisers can recommend several phrases and keywords to target potential clients and businesses.

2. **The Display Network.** This network is more visual with ads (especially banner ads) that are literally all over the internet. Visual banners are an excellent choice for advertisers whose main goal is not necessarily like those of PPC ads which are conversion-driven.

A Massive Audience

Google's advertising platform has an immense reach, and this is among the main advantages of Google. With each passing year, Google progresses on its technology and it gets more sophisticated as it goes. The search volume is likely to become more amazing, especially with

Google's proprietary artificial intelligence such as RankBrain. When this happens, advertisers will also acquire potential users and clients. This potential will make Google a lucrative addition to an advertiser's marketing strategy. It is easy to see why AdWords is the most popular form of online advertising that is used on the PPC platform.

A Level Playing Field

A lot of people think that the advertiser with the largest advertising budget has the best advertising gains with Google ads. But that's not true. In fact, nothing can be further from the truth. The quality of the ads and their relevance is what AdWords focuses on and not so much on how much is spent by advertisers.

Users will continue utilizing Google to search for the things and events they like when they are familiar with the tool and the ads are relevant to the user. Because of this chain reaction, Google AdWords reacts to relevant and quality above monetary input. In this position, advertisers will work on ads that are optimized, relevant, and high quality, rather than the poorly made ads.

The amount advertisers need to bid will depend highly on the relevance and quality of the ads. Google has some metrics that are highly valued apart from click-through rates which are a well-thought-out and reliable assessment of ads' overall appeal and quality.

A Variety of Ad Formats to Choose

AdWords only had 350 advertisers when it was initially launched in 2000. These text-based ads were, at best, rudimentary alongside Google's search results, but the essential elements are still utilized in current ads. PPC and AdWords ads are largely text-based.

With these types of ads, advertisers can have more exciting, compelling, and attractive ads to attract prospective users.

Site links, ad extensions, and social proofing such as location targeting, user reviews, and a slew of other amazing elements are available to advertisers and it offers advertisers unparalleled levels of control and customization.

The other feature Google has introduced is ad formats which cater to specific businesses like hotels, spas, restaurants, workshops, vehicle manufacturers, or computer stores. The advertising needs in some industries go beyond simple text-based ads. They also need ads with rich visual elements such as interactive map data or even high-resolution images.

There is a good chance there will be an ad feature no matter where you sell from or what you sell or to whom, that will make your products reach your desired target market. As Google continues to implement new ad formats and features, it will continue exporting marketers and advertisers to reach newer target audiences and drive their businesses to greater horizons.

The Advantages and Strengths of Facebook Ads

Facebook Ads, compared to Google AdWords, is a newcomer to the online advertising scene, but it has been refining and improving its solutions over the past years. Despite its newcomer status, Facebook Ads is now a pioneer in online advertising, especially in the area of paid social, and has become the norm in digital marketing strategies.

Unmatched Audience Granularity

At this point, Facebook can now proudly claim to have a vast international audience all over the world. There will be no rivals to

Facebook in terms of the size of its audience since almost one-fifth of the earth's population is on Facebook.

Users share almost every detail of their lives on this platform, from marrying to meeting people, the food they eat, their children, and even career moves. From joys to accomplishments to milestones, Facebook users post about these things daily. They also search for and engage with content that aligns with their personal beliefs, interests, values, and ideologies, thus giving advertisers a unique opportunity to create advertising messages that best fit their target audiences in ways we never thought possible.

Among the most powerful features is the ability that allows advertisers to create "lookalike audiences." Customer information can be uploaded from the advertiser's databases to Facebook, and this information can then be filtered based on its own data and information, and delivered by third-party data brokers, to match users that the advertisers uploads.

This creates the "lookalike audience." Advertisers can sufficiently and effectively grow their possible reach of each ad by focusing on customers that show similar behaviors and interests shown by current users. The answer, by now should be clear. Yes, Facebook Advertising works extremely well and is beneficial. However, advertisers should not be viewing Facebook as a billboard but as a gateway to achieving a closer connection to their customers.

A Visual Platform

The other main difference between Facebook Ads and text-based Google AdWords is that Facebook thrives on beautiful images. In fact, it's not Facebook alone. Almost every social media today thrives on beautiful, visual content. The best ads on Facebook blend in beautifully with images and videos and other visual content. Powerful visuals enable advertisers to leverage strong and persuasive images and also make ads with the potential of going viral that are compelling, and high-quality which convey strong messages.

Facebook constantly experiments and evaluates the various ways they can offer better and more superior marketing needs to its advertiser, and a more rewarding and satisfying online experience for its users.

Incredible ROI

Marketers and advertisers using Facebook Ads are often in awe of the scale and level of detail of Facebook's targeting options, combined with the tools they have, for creating engaging and beautiful ads. Apart from that, the ROI (Return On Investment) on these ads is immense. Advertisers can definitely expand their ad budget to its maximum potential and get their money's worth on this platform. The ad campaigns on Facebook, however, are reliant on different factors such as messaging, scope, campaign objectives, and target audience. They areaffordable and gives advertisers the kind of impact needed. The best part is the very specific and direct targeting it allows.

Facebook Ads' highly competitive pricing and amazing potential returns make it a very popular platform for small businesses and companies that have limited budgets. No doubt, Facebook Ads is the best online advertising solution for marketers and advertisers who value their investments.

Google Ad Words vs Facebook Ads: Where to Invest?

Google AdWords and Facebook Ads are powerful platforms for advertising, and suitable for almost every type of business in our 21st-century world. Both of these platforms should be seen as complementing each other in your advertising arsenal. This is important to take note of because many people approach digital marketing with an "either or" attitude when deciding between Facebook ads and Google Adwords. Both have a very important place in a digital marketer's tool belt.

Both the power of paid social and paid search should be utilized by advertisers in order to achieve more successful ads. An advertiser should have two advertising strategies in place that use the benefits of each platform. Marketing messages are best when kept consistent on Facebook Ads and Google AdWords. It is also important to understand how to tailor these messages, so you maximize the ROI and ensure business growth.

Facebook vs AdWords: What's Right for Your Business?

The good old days of PPC advertising were simple—you needed to get clicks on your ads to get money. For early adopters, AdWords was a game changer in online advertising—the traffic was good, the cost was even better. But over the past 10 years, the cost per click on AdWords has increased. In essence, AdWords can make you tons of money, but it can also make you lose loads of money.

As we know today, AdWords is not the only available and viable PPC solution. You have plenty of options where PPC advertising is concerned. So which one should you choose? Of the available options out there—Twitter, LinkedIn, Facebook, and AdWords, you should start with both AdWords and Facebook.

But which one is the right one for your business?

B2B Marketing

Let's begin with B2B (Business-2-Business) marketing. For B2B companies, AdWords works fantastically. B2B searches also incur high CPC (Cost-Per-Clicks), but the customer LTV (Lifetime Value) is also pretty high. You could pay $15-$25 for each click, but if the sale is $10,000, then that is a CPC you can handle. Another beneficial acquisition channel is LinkedIn Ads but for now, the main brands we are looking at are Google and Facebook.

Facebook has also entered the B2B domain because it now also lets you create ads that can be refined to Job Title, Industry, Company Size, Job Role, Seniority, and Office Type. As an added benefit, you can also create lead ads which Facebook auto-populates with the user's contact information and allows you to add at least three additional fields to further identify the lead for your sales team.

For some companies though, these features also enable Facebook ads to become a better fit for their B2B efforts in advertising since these companies are mostly interested in generating top-of-funnel leads. In B2B advertising, the brunt of your budget will go to Adwords and LinkedIn but you should still portion off some of your budget for Facebook Advertising. The quality of B2B traffic and leads you get through Facebook, however, will be significantly lower than what you would receive from AdWords.

Retargeting

Despite how much advertising focus you place on Google or Facebook for your B2B, you must always remember to retarget on these platforms. You have already generated a significant amount of traffic to your site. You can continue this position of staying at the top of your user's mind during the sales process by simply retargeting. For both these platforms, it is always best to use different ads, so you do not end up with ad fatigue. With Facebook, in particular, it is also good to use a range of ad types such as video, single image, GIFs, and carousels, so that your ads are entertaining and fresh.

Facebook vs AdWords

The use of Facebook or AdWords for B2B is straightforward. You can start by investing 90% of your advertising budget on AdWords and the balance 10% on Facebook Ads. Allow the cost per lead and also ultimately cost per sale data decide on what that ratio would be.

B2C Marketing

When it comes to B2C (Business-to-Consumer), Facebook is the better option because of the cost-per-click. In B2B marketing, your LTV can easily absorb a substantially high CPC. However, with B2C advertising, it is much more cost-sensitive.

The cost-per-click for a B2C business on average would be $0.90. On the other hand, clients do pay around $8.00 for clicks on AdWords. Advertising on Facebook for B2C business is the same as going back to the days when Google clicks only cost pennies.

However, with Facebook traffic being higher-funnel-traffic compared to AdWords traffic, your Facebook conversion rate is also typically lower than your AdWords conversion rate. Despite that, your CPC is significantly lower on Facebook than with AdWords.

Where Facebook May Not Be the Best Option

In B2B, you'll find that Adwords campaigns usually perform better than Facebook campaigns, despite Facebook being a great option for B2C businesses. This also depends on the type of products and services you're marketing and the businesses you're marketing to. An exception might be small businesses and sole proprietorships. If you're marketing to small businesses and entrepreneurs, Facebook ads may perform better for you than Adwords.

Niche Products

It is a little difficult to make niche products excel on Facebook simply because Facebook marketing is as good as the data you provide. The target market for niche products is typically small regardless of which part of the funnel you're advertising in. Even when your ads get plenty of clicks on your niche product, you probably won't see the kind of sales conversions you want because Facebook's algorithm does not have that much data to work with.

Who sees your ads is dependent on Facebook's algorithm. So, the smaller your target audience is, the more difficult it will be for Facebook to drive the kind of traffic you desire and get the conversions you want through your Facebook ads. That said, Facebook is not a bad platform for niche products but between Facebook Ads and AdWords, the clear winner for higher ROI would be AdWords.

Expensive Products

Facebook clicks and conversions are thought to be impulsive decisions. People may see your ad but are not necessarily searching for your product. This is ideal if you are selling $30 earrings, but what if it's a new car?

While people will end up buying a new car, they are not necessarily looking for it on Facebook. People aren't typically on Facebook to shop. But if someone is searching for "new Toyota Hilux" on Google, chances are, they are ready to buy. The more expensive the product, the harder it is to get people to buy using Facebook Ads. They will likely click on your ad, but it does not necessarily turn into sales leads.

Allow Data to Decide

Weighing the pros and cons and reviewing the research for themselves, marketers should make the decision on which platform works best for them based on the data and the unique needs of their individual businesses. Your ROIs on your ads should be the deciding factor on how much to invest and how often to invest in Facebook Ads and AdWords.

Generally speaking, Google adwords will cost more and require a bigger budget, but they'll offer a better ROI. But if your customers are usually on Facebook, then that could be a more attractive option. Advertising on Facebook, despite the lower ROI, may get you into other essentials such as building brand awareness which then increases the additional search volume for ads through AdWords.

So, Which is Right for Your Business?

There are plenty of factors that lead to deciding which pay-per-click platform is the most suitable for your business and brand, but if you want to have some considerations, there are things that you can look into:

- B2B Businesses: Good to begin with AdWords and start to retarget on both Facebook and AdWords Display Network. Also, test Facebook for your business by investing at least 10-20% of your monthly ad budget.

- B2C Businesses: Good to begin with Facebook, unless your product is expensive, or it is a niche. In this case, start with AdWords and progress to Facebook. You also need to spend at least 10-20% of your ad budget to test on your non-primary market.

Chapter 2: Defining your Advertising Goals and Objectives

You need to look closely at the overall requirements of your business to create a successful online marketing strategy. In plenty of cases, an internet marketing strategy's effectiveness is undermined by a failure to measuring the elements that are required to understand the scale of success.

In this chapter, we will teach you to measure the efficacy of your current digital marketing strategy.

What Types of Campaigns are you Doing?

There are different outcomes for each type of internet marketing campaign. These outcomes will vary depending on different variables like the targeted customers, products, nature of the company, demographics, environment, and so on. You would have to ensure that marketing campaigns, newsletter campaigns, online advertising campaigns, and social media campaigns are all running concurrently.

You must know the types and number of campaigns that you will run. When you do these campaigns, you must concentrate on the budget for every campaign, its target audience, and so on.

How to measure the efficacy of your campaigns:

For every campaign that you run, it is crucial to measure its effectiveness. Almost all marketing campaigns need to be self-sustaining. This depends entirely on the approach used in digital marketing. You always need to remember that ineffective marketing campaigns can lead to financial loss, waste of resources and damage to your value proposition.

A marketer should measure the campaign's effectiveness against the company's achievements and fixed goals. For example, you can evaluate the growth rate of your business and measure how you compare against your competitors accordingly. Find your brand's value proposition, strategies for growth, goals, and marketing channels, as well as any under-utilized methods. See which of these best fits your requirement and profile.

What Tools do you use to Calculate the ROI of Your Campaigns?

ROI, or return on investment, is viewed as proof of the effectiveness of your marketing plan. Using a few simple tools can easily measure the ROIs. Also, using metrics usually can help measure ROI from:

- Customers: The most important entity for a successful business. Check and keep track of your customer conversion rates. The rate of returning visitors to a site is also essential to maintaining popularity and effectiveness of your campaigns.

- Conversion rates: This is the first element you need to look at. You need to define targets for online purchases, web visits, contact forms, newsletter subscriptions, and time spent on a page as well as user interaction on the site and user interaction on social media.

- Traffic: Measuring referral sources to check which strategies work efficiently through Google Analytics.

- Leads: Check your traffic from your blogs and websites and see which of these converts to leads. Focus on:
    - Bounce Rate.
    - Average page views per visit.
    - Average time spent on site.

- Audits: Social media audits also need to be conducted to measure reach as well as content effectiveness.

- Reach: Track to see how far and wide your posts and content are reaching, is the reach within your target audiences and is traffic resulting from this reach.

- Conversion Regularity: Keep track of the visit-to-lead conversions such as online traffic from leads.

- Costs: Costs to acquire customers or costs per lead is an important factor to measuring campaign effectiveness. Costs can be calculated by dividing the advert costs by the marketing costs with new and paying users that you have acquired during that period.

- A/B tests: Among the best processes to measure campaign effectiveness.

How do we Conduct A/B tests to Measure Effectiveness of Campaigns?

Decide what to test

Using A/B Testing allows you to test two pieces of content against each other. You can test something as minor as the color used for a CTA (Call-To-Action) to something as significant as a redesigned website page. When conducting A/B tests, you must only attribute the results to every piece of content that you are testing as a whole and not on individual or singular differences.

For example, if you are testing two versions of one landing page against each other, and you have made changes to the CTA copy, the form length, the images, and the heading on one of the landing pages, then you cannot attribute that landing page's success to the form itself. You have to attribute the success of it to all four elements that you have changed.

There are many items you can conduct A/B testing on. Let's take a look at what happens when running A/B Testing on what changing the colors of the CTA buttons can do.

Determine the Outcome of Your Test and Decide how you Want to Measure it.

To run an effective A/B test, you have to first identify the goal or result you want from the testing. When it comes to the colors of the buttons, let's assume your goal is measuring the effects of each CTA color on the response of the user who encounters the button. This is among the most straightforward tests that you can conduct. You can easily test this more than once with different colors. You can also test to see how changing the color would make it more visible on your website's real estate. In this example, we will look at the number of clicks on the CTA that send people to the landing page, as a success metric.

Set Your Control and Treatment

The control refers to Version A of your testing. This encompasses the usual elements that you use on a landing page, your CTA, your heading, and your email. Version B is the test subject. It includes the elements and changes that you want to test on. For example, the elements in Version A could be dark blue or light grey, which are standard colors used in most CTAs and blogs. However, in Version B, you want to change the color to bright green.

Create Your A/B test and Publish it live

Once you are done designing your experiment and deciding how it is going to work, it is now time to make it. Create the content for both Version A and Version B. In this example, Version A is the light grey button and Version B is the bright green button. The only difference in this example is the color. The images and copy used on both CTAs are the same. This way, we can only test the effects of the color and its correlation to the number of clicks.

Once this is done, you have to set up the test in your marketing software. Depending on the type of tool you use, the A/B testing can vary in its steps and it also differs according to the type of content to be tested. Here are some of the most common tools for A/B testing:

- Unbounce

- VWO
- Google Analytics Experiments
- Five Second Test
- Convert Experiment
- Maximiser
- Adobe Target
- AB Tasty

Promote Your Test to a Specific Audience

If you want your test to be statistically significant, you will need to promote your content extensively. Send your email and notifications out to a large list and promote your landing page across your social networks and blogs just to get enough people to see your tests.

Bear in mind that these tests are conducted to engage a specific audience, so you need to keep your promotions tailored to only that target market. For instance, you want to see if your Facebook followers will like something on a landing page, so only promote your content on your Facebook account but do not promote your A/B testing content anywhere else except on Facebook.

Gather data Until it's Significant

Once the testing is out, the waiting game begins. You need to consistently promote your test until it has reached a statistically large number. This is important because you can prove that your tests aren't determined by just chance alone. Once you have hit a significant number, you can see if Version B is more efficient than Version A.

But what happens if you never hit a statistical significance? You need to continue pushing promotions and wait it out for a few more days. Some A/B testing takes up to 30 days just to acquire enough traffic to obtain significant results. However, if after a month during which you've experienced significant traffic, you still have not seen any major results, then this testing hasn't made any huge impact on conversions. It is time to move on to a different type of testing.

Investigate Your Entire Marketing Funnel

If your experiment worked, great! But it isn't the end. It is time to look outside the test's original intention to see if it has any other effect on any other part of your marketing channels.

Some of the smallest details for a website or blog are some of the most effective in changing perceptions, increasing conversion rates, and so on. You may think that colors do not have any significant impact, but your tests show you that they do. You can also take your metrics one step further by looking at closed-loop analytics. With these, you can track to check if people who clicked on the CTA have turned into paying customers. Maybe the bright green call to action makes people become customers faster.

By looking at other factors beyond your massive campaigns, you can discover that an A/B test has other impacts and effects that you were not anticipating. If those impressions were good, then you can focus your attention even more on them. If they are not good, then you might want to change them.

Always remember that A/B testing can have larger implications than just the metrics alone.

Iterate on Your Findings

You have just finished your first A/B test, but do not stop there. There's so much more you can test. For example, in our CTA test, apart from changing the color, we can also change the location of the CTA on our website. Alternatively, modifying the copy of the CTA could also be done to see how users respond to it and click on it. You can also run your CTA of the same kind on a different timeline, date, during a holiday, and such so you can see the responses it brings. Testing your site can always help you tweak your campaigns and, in turn, bring in better conversion rates.

Simple Steps for Effective Online Marketing Strategies

1. Targets

In any marketing campaign, the first move is always to identify what your targets are. It is always good to focus on two primary goals and then two minor ones. All of these goals have to be ethical, have a timeline, easy to achieve, comply with the needs of the moment, and must be unique to the company.

2. Objectives

Setting specific marketing objectives keeps you focused on your goals. You can track your goals and accomplishments better by centralizing certain measurement metrics. For example, you will need a metric that determines the likes you receive on a successful target if increasing and influencing sales is one of your marketing objectives. Objectives can be categorized by measurability indexes, relevancy, and time.

3. Identification

Apart from defining your marketing aims and goals, it is also crucial to know your consumer's demographics and other essential profile information. For example, if you are conducting a community program, then it might be better to work on social network campaigns. If your target is the more mature groups, email marketing or even conventional marketing would do the trick and save you time and effort. Knowing your target market is very crucial for creating an online marketing strategy that has optimal results.

4. Market Identifiers

For any campaign, it is always good to stay ahead of your competition. If you know your competition is gearing up for a 50% discount sale for the holiday season, then don't be outsmarted by this. Tweak your campaign to offer promotions and discounts too.

5. Platforms

Pick and choose your social media. In any marketing campaign, overdoing your social media networks could mean death to your campaign. Before signing up and opening accounts for every network, understand your target group and choose your social media appropriately. Apart from that, choosing when to advertise on social media is also essential. For example, adults may engage more on social media during lunch hours or after work compared to teens who probably engage in social media longer.

6. Content Strategies

A good content strategy is valuable when combined with a proficient marketing strategy. Three vital components for content strategy are the number of posts per day/week, the time of day, and content type. There are periods of time that are suited for the types of social media posts. It is important to use this strategy and information when posting your products, service, or brand.

7. Marketing Techniques

As mentioned earlier in this chapter, tracking your marketing strategies has immense benefits. Tracking measures enable a marketer to identify what works and what falls short. Improvements can be made when we track our goals and objectives.

Chapter 3: Finding & Evaluating Your Niche & Your Audience

What is Niche Marketing?

Niche marketing is all about focus. It is a focus on selling and advertising your strategies towards a targeted portion of the market. You do not market to everyone who could benefit from your product or service. Your niche targets to specific people, focusing exclusively on a group of people or a demographic section of likely customers that would most definitely enjoy or benefit from your products.

Niche sectors stand out because of these reasons:
- Geographic area
- Lifestyle
- Occasion
- Profession
- Style
- Culture
- Activity or habits
- Behavior
- Demographic
- Need
- Feature reduction or addition

Niche marketing's biggest benefit would be that it allows brands to stand out from the pack and appear as unique. This ensures that your message resonates better with its already unique and distinct customer section. To build a lasting and strong relationship with your target audience and reach a higher growth potential, a brand should not blend in but instead be more valuable and stand out by employing niche marketing initiatives.

Finding Specific Niches Using Facebook Advertising

Facebook has over 1.5 billion active monthly users. With this power, they can easily market to whomever they want. This is a huge opportunity for marketers and advertisers. But not everything is be perfect. Despite all that, some advertisers still find it hard to match their messages with the right audience.

While it is a good start to define your location, age, and gender for your ads, there is actually plenty more that you can do with Facebook Ads.

Here are other ways you can create a niche marketing using Facebook:

New Generations

In this era, you want to target the millennials and baby boomers. This group of audience is ideal for fashion, gadgets, clothing, and gaming.

People with an Upcoming Anniversary

Have something new to sell? You can reach to a target audience that is celebrating a special day such as an anniversary of any kind—work, birthday, or wedding. These groups are great for selling greeting services, flower deliveries, event planners, recreational activities, holidays, and restaurants.

People who have High Technology Adoption

If you are selling something that is either too high-tech or the opposite, target your audience following their technology exposure.

Niches by Household Members

You can also target your ads to hit people who live with a

family member or have separate households. These groups are perfect for selling kitchen accessories, furniture, home appliances, and cleaning services.

Friends of People with Anniversary

We targeted people who are celebrating an upcoming anniversary but what about their friends and family? A reminder that a loved one's anniversary is coming up is the perfect time to sell online gift stores, eCards, eGreetings, party suppliers, and greeting services. These people are usually friends and family of the people who have upcoming birthdays and anniversary celebrations.

Small Business Owners

Small business owners are among the biggest groups or pages in Facebook. You can reach a wide demographic of customers if you are in the insurance sector, banking, or just selling your products and services on a small scale such as web hosting, web designing, and even small-time catering.

Target People who have a New Job

Target those who have landed a job! You can target them if you are selling clothing (they need office wear!), fashion, online learning platforms, management software, and eBooks.

People in new Relationships

You can create a niche for your advertising by narrowing it down to target people that have recently become engaged or just got married! You can sell greeting services, bouquet deliveries, flowers, eCards, event management, and restaurants.

People that create Events on Facebook

You can target people that have recently created an event on Facebook because this can be a great business for event management companies and party planners. This is also great for caterers, party supply companies, decorators, music and entertainment providers, and booking and registration services.

People who have Traveled Recently

People who have just returned from traveling can bring in big business especially for post-holiday services such as photo albums, photo editing software, GoPro video editing software, and graphic icons. You can also advertise medical services for those who have returned back from holidays as well.

Soon-to-be Parents

Couples who are about to be new parents will have loads of things to buy from baby strollers, baby toys, books, and also looking into preschool admissions and insurance. This is a major target audience that you can target for your niche marketing.

Reach People Using Facebook Payments Platform

This niche is a must-have for a business that is selling on Facebook or has linked third-party paid apps to Facebook. This feature enables marketers to reach all the audiences that have recently made a payment or are high spenders or people that have used the payment feature at least once. This is great for app developers, e-commerce sites, online retailers, as well as Facebook pages that sell stuff.

People Based on Their Technology Interest

Targeting people based on their interest in technology is the ideal way to ensure that these groups get the messages you want them to know. If you are selling computer devices, or you are launching a new app, or having a discount sale on consumer electronics, these are the kinds of things people, who like and use tech tools and gadgets, will want to know. Advertisers from the cell phone industry, computer hardware or software as well as e-commerce stores can fine-tune their marketing strategy to hit these customers.

People Based on their Political Interests

Facebook Ads can definitely help you segment out and reach audiences based on their political alignment. This is great for marketers who want to send out political party events, meetings, town hall discussions, and media houses.

Users Based on the Browsers they use

Browsers are one of the main ways Facebook knows what you are searching for. You can target your ads based on what browser your audience usually uses, whether it is a safari extension or a chrome extension. This is extreme laser targeting and would be useful for developer tools, browser extension developers, and productivity apps.

Users who have Responded to Your Event

People who are interested and answered to your event definitely means they like something about your event and may be interested in similar events. If you are an event creator, trade show organizer, or webinar organizer, you can create your niche with this audience type.

Users Based on Their Email Domain

You can also use Facebook Ads to target people using specific email domains such as Gmail or Yahoo or AOL. This is perfect for advertisers who sell auto-responders, email apps, or email marketing apps.

Target People Living Away from Home

There's always that group of people you can target that are away from home and homesick. There are many services that can benefit people who are living away from home such as money transfer businesses, fashion, travel, airline ticketing agencies, and e-greetings. Even immigration consultants can benefit from niche marketing like this.

Mobile Devices by Brand

Mobile device targeting is a must for any marketer as it enables you to target audience based on the type of mobile device they are using. This is ideal for mobile accessories stores, mobile app developers, as well as cell phone companies.

Friends of Users That Like Your Page

Birds of a feather flock together, no? The likelihood of a person engaging with your ad if their friend has also engaged with it is high. Utilize Facebook Connections Targeting to focus on this niche of targeting people who are friends of the people who like your page. Page owners of any kind of business will benefit from this kind of niche targeting.

Evaluating the Profitability of Your Audience

Tip #1 – Brainstorming:

Brainstorming is always effective for practically anything you need to work on—ideas, solutions, methods, and finding the right niche. To begin brainstorming ideas for your niches, meet up with your business partner or like-minded friends, who will be able to help you or someone you trust. Friends and family, who know you and your business partner are ideal. Next, you want to block off time to focus on your brainstorming; set a meeting, time, and date for this.

When you meet, one of the things to think about is the items that you or your business partner or friends have bought online or recently purchased. Write these things down, even if it perplexes you. There will be tons of niches that are profitable but that does not mean you should rush into the business of dropshipping.

When you have your niches, write them down and filter them according to:

- Competition: Look out for other competitor stores and look into the kinds of products that are oversaturated.
- Loyalty: Look at how users interact with brands they are loyal with. Scan comment sections because there are bound to be users who comment how long they have been using a product or service.

Tip #2 - Research, compare, and evaluate trends

eBay is one of the places to check whether items sell online. Once you get onto eBay, one of the things you want to research is identifying products in the different niches in higher-priced bracket, the ones that are expensive, so it can be anything like $50 or $200 or $500 depending on the product. When you get your search results, allow it to show "completed listings." Completed lists shows items in red or green, red being the item did not sell and green is sold. Look at the items only for the ads you are considering to niche in. It is okay to go over this list a few times until you identify about 20 products within your niche that sell out almost always, at least 10 units a day.

Tip #3 - Utilize Amazon

Being the world's largest retailer, Amazon sells everything imaginable. Because of this, Amazon is one of the best tools on the Internet for evaluating your ad and other amazing possibilities that you never thought of. Amazon is also a great place to help you in a specific niche as well by identifying the ad that sells the best. You can also choose "best sellers" from the navigation bar located at the top of the page right under the search bar. You can see all the ads that are shown or the products that are currently selling the best.

Tip #4 - Put on your Marketer Cap

You want to make a profit for any kind of venture or business you are in. So, you will most likely look into ads that create a successful profit line. To help discover what your target audience is talking about, here are some questions you can ask:
- What kind of blogs and websites do they interact with and visit the most?
- What kind of pages or accounts do they follow on social media?
- Which online stores do they usually purchase from?
- What do you think are their biggest obsessions?
- What kind of products do they usually collect or buy most frequently?

Tip #5 - Google Trends

Yes, Google Trends is another tool you can use to evaluate if your niche is profitable. What you want to look out for are niches that have stable growth, no matter how slight. Here is a list you can check out on Google Trends.

Tip #6 - FB Search

Facebook search can help determine the amount of engagement your posts actually get. You can also use this as a competitor analysis tool, so you can see what kind of posts both your competitors as well as customers make. You can also look up at the brands that are within your niche. Search using specific keywords.

Your search will turn up information based on people, pages, photos, videos, links, and marketplace. When you look at these pages, you can see the number of followers. It will also help you understand the kind of frequency your Facebook posts need to be following, which is somewhere between 1-2 posts per day to have a competitive advantage and scale quickly. Browsing the pages that come up in your search also gives you an idea of the direction of your marketing strategy. Looking through photos helps you understand the kind of material you need to create and the markets you can target.

Continue Your Research

You want to make sure you have an audience for your niche even before you were spending hours marketing and buying ads online. Here's a quick list of what to look for:

- What kind of social platforms do people market your niche on?
- Are there dedicated Facebook groups for your niche?
- Are there targeting options you can use on Facebook for this niche?
- What kind of forums exist for people to discuss the niche?
- Do people host events for this niche?
- Do influencers post about this niche?
- Are there fans for your niche?

Pinterest, YouTube, Instagram, and of course, Facebook, are all popular places to look if your niches are talked about on these platforms. It is always better to put your content where it is seen, heard, and speaks because this is where your audience spends time.

Another thing is, all these platforms have one element in common. They are all heavy on visuals which means, stunning images and video reach out to your audience faster.

Tools to Use to Evaluate the Profitability of Your Niches

A. Checking on Amazon for Profitable Niches

With Amazon, you can see the number of reviews a product gets which is a huge sign that it is profitable. All you need to do is enter your own niche and ideas and see what the results give you. If there are tons of products with plenty of reviews, that is a good sign your product and your ad will be seen. It is said that for every 1 review seen on Amazon, that translates to 10 to 1000 people having purchased the product because not everyone is going to write a review.

Take note of the average number of reviews the customer has on a product on the first page itself. This is for reference later, so you can craft an ad that speaks to your customers. Ideal markets are the ones that do not have one single product to sell but have plenty of options you can give your customers over and over again. Look for related products that you may be able to sell again too. Put in the ideas and take note of what product type sells best based on the reviews they get. This will help you in promoting your own products later.

B. Checking ClickBank for Profitability

If your niche is includes digital products, you can also use Clickbank.com to check your profitability. As the largest retailer of digital products on the internet, ClickBank can show you how many products out there match your digital niche. When you search for a product, write down the number of searches you get for reference purposes. Look also for the type of digital products people are purchasing such as info-products, eBooks, software, and even memberships. If you see 3 to 4 products in your searches, it is enough to know that there is a demand.

You can also look for "Gravity" on ClickBank. The Gravity number is a unique ClickBank algorithm that calculates the number of unique affiliates that have sold at least one item of the product in the past 7 days. The higher the number of gravity, the more affiliates there are promoting and making sales.

This tells you that the product is profitable and also popular. When you see loads of products in the niche you are in which also has high gravity score, this shows you that affiliates, like yourself, are making money off this product.

C. Finding Profitable Affiliate Programs on ShareASale

ShareASale is an affiliate network that enables independent companies to run affiliate programs. This allows consumers to also promote their products. You would need to sign up and verify your account before you can start using their site to browse affiliate programs. Once you are in ShareASale, you can find over 1,000 affiliate programs from independent merchants that include big names such as ModCloth, Reebok, NFL, OptinMonster, and many more. Click on Merchants, then Search for Merchants, and you can enter your niche idea in your search box. Click on products before clicking the blue button. You can then see the number of products and the merchants related to your niche. If you see plenty of merchants and tons of products, then you've found a profitable niche.

D. Using Commission Junction to Check for Profitable Niches

Also known as CJ.com, this is quite similar to ShareASale. This site also allows businesses to host their affiliate program. Here, you can see big brands such as VistaPrint, TripAdvisor, Verizon, and Zappos. This website also requires you to verify your business and sign up.

Click on "Advertisers" and then key in your niche idea in the "keyword" box. Just like the ShareASale site, if you see thousands of retailers and numerous products related to your searched keywords, then you have a goldmine staring back at you. This shows there's a customer demand.

E. How to Use Google to Find Other Signs of Profitability

Of course, Google is also a great place to find products that are profitable. You can also find products on sale which may not turn up in your research using the affiliate networks. You can search for something like "niche + affiliate program," niche being the product of your choice, and see what the results bring you.

F. How to Use OfferVault to Validate Your Niche Ideas

One way to validate your niche ideas is to use www.offervault.com where you can also search for affiliate programs that are within your niche and see the CPA (cost per acquisition) offers. CPA offers mean you are being paid for sending a lead, or in other words getting customer's information rather than making a sale. This is a different thing altogether, but for now you can use this to search your niche and see the results that come out. Not every niche is a good product for CPA offers, so there may be a chance you will not see your product here. But do not be discouraged. Some networks show the same products while some show different things depending on the algorithm of the site.

G. Are Products on Sale?

When you see certain products on sale and you see them on many different networks, these are signs that these products are selling well. This also means you have a profitable niche, and you can definitely make money from it. This also means that investing in ads on Facebook will enable Facebook to pull out as much data as possible to reach your target audience.

Conclusion

Now you need to go through all data from whatever you have been researching and all the positive signs you have gathered. When you look at these factors, the numbers will give you a very conclusive idea of whether the market you are in is profitable. Profitable niches usually have these common traits:

- High levels of people searching for your niche.
- Plenty of products that sell well.
- Plenty of people paying to advertise said niche.
- Loads of activity online from forums, blogs, Facebook groups, and other social media chatter.

There is money to be made if you see these positive results.

Chapter 4: Paid Ads vs. Creating Free Content on Facebook

Facebook Ads vs. Boosted Posts: Which Should You Choose?

This question is very common among the admins of Facebook pages. Even if you are new to a page, you are bound to see Facebook's prompt to "boost a post." This usually comes in when Facebook detects high activity on a certain post or if its algorithms have found other pages with similar content boosting a certain type of content that matches yours. The ability to boost your post is a very simplified addition to Facebook Ads' system. This system is designed to be simple and easy to use even for a non-marketer or advertiser.

However, simple doesn't always mean better. Boosted posts come at the cost of significant customization the complete ad system provides. In this chapter, let's look at the difference between boosted posts of Facebook campaign ads so you can decide which is best for your business and when to use paid ads.

Why Have Boosted Posts on Facebook?

With boosted posts, advertisers have the choice to use a post that has already been posted any time and promote it. When boosting a post, page admins can choose their target audience, decide on a budget, and how long the boosted post should run. This can be done on any post on your Page's timeline.

Facebook Ads vs Boosted Posts

A post that is boosted focuses on increased visibility for that particular post and more engagement. Boosted posts are great for brand awareness., and an increase in engagement can add value to social proof. An increase in engagement can also mean a lower CPA or CPA. You could also end up with more results with the same value of the investment.

With Facebook's recent update, you not only can increase engagement for that particular post, you can also choose the outcome of it, whether you want people to visit your profile more or visit your site. If this is your option, compared to increasing engagement on the post in terms of likes or comments, your ad should be visible to people who will most likely end up clicking. This option is available only if your boosted post has a link in it.

Changing the Objective of the Ad

Boosting posts right now is much simpler, and Facebook admins do not have or need to make many choices. For smaller businesses, who make up a big percentage of Facebook pages, this is preferable. With a few simple clicks, you already have a boosted post.

Boost Posts Interface

Boosted posts are much more limited than the full Facebook Ads system. There are some other things that you need to do on Facebook Ads compared to boosted posts. This includes:
- Having plenty of objective options.

It is important to define what your ad objective is at the start as this will help you determine what your campaign should be about. Posts that are boosted will allow you to focus on whether you want to increase engagement or increase website clicks. On the other hand, full systems will allow you to determine a specific objective whether it is conversions, store visits, or lead generation. Boosted posts do not allow for these types of campaign objectives.
- Campaign types.

Identifying your campaign types is imperative because Facebook will use this info to focus your ads on users who have the higher likelihood of taking the kind of action you are optimizing your

ad for. This is determined based on the user's history of activity.
- Choosing detailed placement options.

When you decide on boosted posts, you can uncheck or check an Instagram placement whether on desktop or mobile. This includes Facebook's side ads and news feeds, Instagram stories and feeds, articles, messenger ads, as well as audience network ads. You can decide if you want your campaign to be shown for desktop users or mobile users only.
- Allowing for more targeting customization.

When it comes to boosted posts, you cannot use multiple audience types. For example, you cannot custom your audience and also add interest targeting. You can do this and so much more using Facebook ads. With Facebook Ads, you can customize by doing the following:

1. **Enabling manual bidding:** You can conduct manual bidding through Facebook Ads. You can choose either a maximum-per-bid rate or a maximum average bid. You can also choose what you want to pay for, whether clicks or impressions. Since you are able to choose these methods to scale your Facebook Ads, this is a significant but small feature to know if you ever choose to use it.
2. **Bid settings:** You can create carousel ads, ad descriptions, ad headlines, and choose the call to action button that would work best for your ads. These are the different creative and formatting options that you can do through Facebook ads but not through boost posts.
3. **Gaining additional creative control:** You can also add in your own headlines and targeted descriptions and choose a CTA that will work efficiently with your ads. These formatting options are not available when it comes to boosted posts.

When to use the full Facebook Ads vs Boosted Posts?

Facebook Ads, about 99% of the time, are the most obvious choice for most marketers as it offers much more flexibility in crafting the right ad to hit the right audience. You can even customize the exact objective you want your ad to achieve, and it can be optimized to give you the results you want.

You can also create video awareness campaigns via Facebook Ads. You can also do retargeting towards the 75% of people who have watched the video and target them with a lead ad that is automatically filled out with their information. Once they become conversions, you can then focus on retargeting users who have visited your site and show them similar items to what they are interested in buying with a carousel ad that has high-conversions.

When should I use boosted posts?

Boosted posts work amazingly in very specific conditions. Here are the circumstances that boosted posts work well:
- When you want to maximize visibility on a specific post.
- When you want to build social proof.
- When you want to create brand awareness.
- When you want to create profile awareness.

Examples on when boosted posts work amazingly well:
- When announcing a specific event and you want to increase attendance for that event as well as do social proofing at the same time.
- When you have a major announcement such as a launch, a release of a product or service, or even a grand opening, and you want more engagement and visibility.

- When you have shared user-generated content and you want to win over customer's trust and gain new followers.

When you need a quick engagement boost to help with your social proofing or if there is a specific message you want users to see, your best bet is boosted posts.

However, if you want a full-fledged ad campaign that gives you better customization to reach a specific and wider group of users and match with your campaign goals, then Facebook Ads is the way to go. There is no right or wrong with using either boosted content or Facebook ads. The only consideration is what your goals and objectives are and matching the right method with the objective you want to achieve.

Pros and Cons of Creating Paid Ads vs. Creating Free Content to Encourage More Organic Growth and Traffic

Let's be honest. It is difficult to get people to your business, whether you are doing this virtually or physically. If only it was that easy to just push a button and the right customers just show up. But alas, life is not that way. It takes effort, intelligence, and pairing the right tools to attract your customers.

Whether it is driving traffic to your site with Google Ads or Facebook Ads, or reaping traffic through social media, blogging, or email marketing, you are paying for your traffic either with money or time, or both.

The question here is not necessary if you want to pay for Organic traffic versus Paid Traffic since you will be paying either way. The ultimate question here is which will be more worth the effort, time, and money.

1 - Pay-Per-Click vs. Organic Traffic

Organic Traffic really just means traffic coming in via organic search. Organic search is only from search engine results. This literally means a user goes on a browser of their choice, looks for whatever product and service they want, and when the search results come in, they then click on whatever links they want, which will direct them to a specific site.

While this is organic, advertisers and marketers can still influence this decision. But most often than not, organic traffic already knows what they want and have made a decision the split second they click on search. It is only a matter of deciding which link to click on.

Pay-Per-Click Traffic, also known as PPC, this traffic is a result of users clicking on an ad that you paid to be placed at a specific location on the internet. Almost every platform or search engine allows you to set up advertising campaigns that you only pay based on the number of times people have clicked on your ad. You decide how much you want to pay and the ad service you use will charge you until the funds you have stipulated run out. You can also set up an ad runtime which charges you based on the clicks that happen during a time period.

The location of the ads or placement is entirely dependent on several factors such as the ad relevance, the bidding process, and the desired audience response. The position your ad takes on a page is directly dependent on the performance of the ad or the bids. Where PPC is concerned, you are simply utilizing a middle person, and in this case, the ad platform to link your website with to the other people who wouldn't access your site.

2 - Organic Traffic Benefits Vs. PPC Traffic Benefits

Most of the time when people use a search engine to look for certain products and services, they do not intend to click on ads. 70% of link searches are usually organic and that is consistent with organic traffic.

Organic Traffic Pros:

Positive Bias: The biggest benefit of organic traffic is that they will click on links that they already trust to find what they need. If you rank high on a search engine result, that means the user already has a positive perception on your site and trust that you are an expert in the industry.

However, you really need to be at the top for this perception to be present. This is where organizations and businesses use SEO to ensure that they are at the top 10 of a search engine result, specifically Google. Google is the gold standard simply because they have a large share of the search engine market. Google creates the SEO rules; other search engines follow suit.

What Google does is weed out spam and give users who use their engine the best content there is. When doing this, Google has consistently improved and changed their filtering system in order to provide the best quality content on the World Wide Web.

The SEO game is built on the quality of a site, its relationships with other websites, as well as the traffic flow to that site. Of course, it is much more than that when it comes to Google algorithms such as quality images and a responsive site. The main focus here is the quality of the content.

Encouraging Improvement: Before you begin an organic traffic campaign, you must already have built a site with great content. When there is no content, there will be no traffic and no search engine result ranking. Your ultimate goal is quality which will keep bringing people to your site, especially if your marketing objective is to be ranked higher in search engine results. SEO enables you to stay high on the ranking list and with better content, you can always be at the top. Great content needs to be on all pages of your site. This will not only optimize your site for search engines but also improve your customer's user experience, satisfaction, and increase brand awareness and favorability.

Organic Traffic Cons:

Time: The cost of organic traffic is, of course, time. You would need to spend a decent amount of time to wait for organic traffic to pick up. People need to know that you exist in order to want to find you. Depending on your strategy for search engine optimization, this can take a few months or even years if you want to be on the first page of search results. You may not have that kind of time to boost your website traffic.

Resources: Organic traffic also requires an immense amount of resources, but the good thing is there are also plenty of free tools on the internet to help you optimize your site to attract organic traffic. Knowing what kind of tools there are and how to use them is essential in your marketing arsenal

PPC Traffic Pros:

PPC traffic is an excellent source of traffic and if you create outstanding paid ads, you will see the kind of traffic build up. It appears that selected top positions will get an average click-through rate of 7%. Those looking for brand specific or product specific searches will also see your ad, which will increase the click-through rate compared to organic traffic.

You can definitely pay an agency to search engine optimize your site. There are plenty of services that do this, but it does take time to see results. However, PPC traffic is faster than unpaid organic traffic. Once you have paid and secured your spot at the topmost ranking, that spot is yours until some other site comes up and has a powerful SEO that pushes you down. Whatever it is, the likelihood of you being at the top 3 or even at the top 10 will still be there unless you stop optimizing your site or doing any other marketing or advertising initiatives.

Tailored fit: The ads that you pay for will also be tailored to meet your objectives and hit the specific audiences. Through PPC ads, you can target your customers as well as potential customers in ways that organic traffic cannot do.

If you do not measure the intent of the user when you pick your keywords for SEO, you probably will not get the kind of customers you want. PPC advertising does reach out to segments that you may not have covered through your organic SEO methods. With PPC, you can target audiences by age, marital status, income even, education level, and even hobbies.

PPC Traffic Cons:

Money: The problem with many things in this world is the lack of money. Without enough budget, your best option to increase traffic is by sticking to organic traffic. If you want to generate tons of leads in a short amount of time, then PPC is the way to go and you need to put in a serious amount of cash for this to happen effectively. However, the great thing with paid ads is that you can turn them off whenever you have what you need.

Both paid and organic are essential to your site. There really isn't the perfect way. Both methods bring in traffic in different ways, and usually a good ad campaign takes advantage of both organic as well as paid traffic to create brand awareness and visibility as well as drive traffic to your site.

Chapter 5: Building a Company Facebook Page

Facebook is one of the most popular free social networking sites that allows users to create profiles, upload content from photos and videos, send messages, poke friends, and keep in touch with other people.

To open an account, all you need to do is go to **www.facebook.com** and click on sign up. Next, put in your first name, surname, an email address, and a password. You are also required to fill in your birthday and identify your gender. Once you're done, Facebook will send a verification email to the email address you provided, you verify your account, and just like that, you are a registered Facebook user!

When we talk about Social Media marketing, Facebook has a special account catered to businesses, and this is called Pages. To open a Facebook page, you must first have a private Facebook account, and in this case, it's the account you opened up earlier. This is your own personal Facebook account—your Pages account is exclusively for your business.

How to open a Facebook Page?

Below is a series of simple steps to follow to open a Facebook page.

Step 1: Choose a Page Type

Head over to **https://www.facebook.com/pages/create.php**. You need to click on what selection best fits your business needs. These types are:

- Local Business or Place.

- Company, Organization, or Institution.

- Brand or Product.

- Artist, Band, or Public Figure.

- Entertainment.

- Cause or Community.

If you are a business that serves your community, then number 1 is your best category, but if your business serves a whole county or the entire world, then number 2 is your category. Since we are talking about Social Media Marketing, for this tutorial, let us focus on option number 2, Company, Organization, or Institution.

When you click on Company, Organization, or Institution, Facebook will require you to specify the type of your company by choosing a category. This can be anything from a political organization, food & beverage, community organization, Preschool, School, Small Business, or Travel and Leisure.

You are also required to provide a company name. We recommend that you follow exactly the business name that you have registered it under. Facebook allows you to only change your business name and URL once, so make sure you make the right choice.

Step 2: Fill in the Basic Information

By completing the first step, Facebook will then automatically walk you through four primary sections of information, which will provide the foundation of your Page. You need to give a short description of your company within two to three sentences. This will be the main introduction to your site. Make sure this information is the same as what is shown on your website or your objectives. The great thing is, the content on the About page can be revised.

Personalize your URL so that it's easier to promote your

Facebook page on other material and sites as well as on your website. A confusingly long URL isn't going to make it. The URL should mirror your Page's name or Business name. For example, if your business is Delia's Homemade Cakes, then your URL can be www.facebook.com.deliascakes

A profile picture is a must. Being a business page, uploading a logo for your business is the right step. Your profile picture will serve as the first visual icon for your page, so make it identifiable and the same with all your other online presence because you want to increase brand recognition. Anything you publish on your page or comment to other sites will have your profile picture. A square image works best, in the size of 180 x 180 pixels.

Fill in your contact details and include a cover photo as well. Once you are done, Facebook will also prompt you to advertise your new page. However, do not do this immediately—regardless of whether a paid advertisement is part of your strategy or not. There is no point having paid advertisement when you do not have compelling content on your page. So, before you click to subscribe, work on getting relevant material on your page first.

Step 3: Getting Acquainted with the Admin Panel

The good thing about Facebook is that it is extremely user-friendly. Once you are done providing all the relevant information, you are one step further in providing a solid foundation for your Page. Your Business Page is now LIVE! But don't share it to your personal feed or suggest it to your friend's list just yet. You do not want to do this until you get good content up.

On your page, look for "Settings." Click it, and you will see two panels. On the left are the various setting categories and on the right are the different items you can edit or change. In here, the most important things you need to change/edit or add are the Page Info, which basically tells people about your business. You can also change the Notifications to determine how you'd like to receive Page alerts.

The most important feature is the Page Roles. This function allows you to decide who the primary manager of the Page should be, and who can be editors or contributors.

Step 4: Adding Strategic Content

When it comes to content, Facebook allows six different types of content uploads which are:

- Plain text status.

- Photo with caption.

- Link with caption.

- Video with caption.

- Event page.

- Location check-in.

For the first post, go with a status update to say hello and perhaps an update on the latest project you are working on. Down the road of your social media marketing campaign, be sure to use a variety of content to engage, educate, and connect with your audience. Once you are done with uploading your profile photo, make sure to update your cover photo too. The cover photo helps attract people to your Page.

Now that you have content on your page, you can invite friends first, and then your colleagues and your acquaintances that you know can create some initial activity. You can also encourage your customers now that you have some form of activity on your page.

Step 5: Measure your Progress

Insights by Facebook are a great tool for Facebook Pages. This feature allows you to monitor the activity of your visitors based on the content you have uploaded. You get to see the page views, page likes, reach, and engagement over a certain period of time. You can also see what type of activity it is:

- Organic: the number of people who visited/clicked/liked/shared/viewed your post without unpaid distribution.

- Paid: the number of people who visited/liked/clicked/shared/viewed your post as a result of viewing your ads.

Insights will also tell you which posts have a higher engagement, reach, and the time with the highest activity. All this valuable data will enable you to craft future messages to target an even greater correspondence. It will also tell you which items work, and which don't. With Insights you can view:

- Overview: This tab shows you the overall activity within a 7-day timeline, such as page likes, post reach, and overall visitor engagement.
- Likes: This tab will show you the growth and losses of your fan base. You will also see the performance of paid posts and organic posts.
- Reach: This tab shows you the organic number of people your posts or page reaches every day. Once a week, check this statistic to see if there are spikes in your data and cross-check it to see what you posted that day.
- Views: This tab tells you where your visitors are coming from, like from another website, an article mentioning your business, another Facebook account, and so on.

And with that, you now have a Facebook Page!

Chapter 6: Biggest Mistakes People Make with Facebook Ads

Facebook advertising campaigns can feel like a Minesweeper Game—sometimes you hit your target and get the gains you want, and sometimes you hit a snag and things don't work out the way you hoped. Sure, it takes trial and error with ads to see which ones work and which don't, but mistakes come at the expense of time and money. So, in this chapter, we will look at rookie mistakes to avoid when it comes to Facebook Ads.

1. Targeting Mistakes

You may have stellar ad copy, a beautifully designed ad, and exceptional ad placement, but if it is seen by an audience that does not want what you have to offer, there will all be for naught. A research conducted by AdEspresso in 2016 found that there is a possibility of over a 1000% difference in the ads' cost-per-click depending on the audience you're targeting. For instance, the cost-per-click (CPC) for some age groups garnered higher percentages than others.

It's always a smart move to begin your Facebook ad campaigns using customer research to ensure that you target the right audience. For example, a leading SEO company called MOZ was able to make one million dollars just because they interviewed their customers the old-fashioned way to understand their needs and thus, improved their product accordingly.

How to Avoid Targeting the wrong Facebook Audience

Do customer research on demographics.

A simple research practice on your customer base to discover the obvious audience demographics, such as job seniority, age, location, education, gender, and even purchasing behavior can tell you a lot. These demographics can be targeted on Facebook. When targeting ads, make sure to remember that you also have to target according to geographic specificity.

Analyze interests—You can also look at Facebook Audience Insights to understand the people who are part of your fanbase Facebook. This tool gives you information that people have expressed on the platform together with the information from reliable third-party apps. When you know the interests of your potential audience, it will become easier to craft relevant messages for your ads and produce a winning ad design.

Target niche interests.

Targeting a wide range of interests instead of focusing on a niche can be detrimental. Best to narrow down your audiences' interests to make it more effective. You can add different layers to the interest so that your audience matches at least one. For example, if you are in the digital education industry, your niches could be: i) digital education resources, ii) teaching resources, iii) online quizzes, iv) interactive games, and v) gamified learning.

2. Low Audience and Offer Match

When crafting your ad messages, you must also consider that not everyone that sees your ad knows your brand. Some audience members are familiar with the benefits of your product but there is a probability that not many ad viewers have heard of your company or brand before. Some of them might ask, "Why am I seeing this ad?"

Your PPC campaign target audience can be summarized into these three different categories:

- People who have never heard of you and have not visited your site.
- People who know who you are but not sure what you do exactly.
- People who have purchased or used your service and product or are at least familiar with your brand, and are on the path of becoming a customer.

Each of the above categories requires a dedicated ad campaign on Facebook so you can hit them in the right spot.

For example, we looked at an ad by a cruise company that wanted to promote a big discount to encourage conversions and attract new customers. The issue here is there was no explanation on what to do with the discount in case someone wanted to use it. The ad makes total sense if the viewer of the ad has interacted with the company before and is aware of its benefits, but to most people, the ad will not make any sense—especially not to any new viewers or users.

A very effective yet simple way that you can evaluate your audience is to check Facebook's Relevance Score, which is a calculated metric that enables marketers and advertisers to understand how an audience reacts to a certain ad.

Adpsresso, when analyzing 104,256 Facebook ads, found that Facebook campaigns' Relevance Score enables marketers to predict both the CPC and click-through rate. Essentially, the higher the ad relevance, the less marketers should pay for conversions and for clicks. You can check your ad's relevance meter when you break down your Facebook reports by performance, as shown in the following image:

3. Targeting Audiences That Are Too Broad

Unless you are a household brand, targeting 20 million people will do more damage than good. Your ad offer, and the copy must be tailored to be relevant to the broader set of people you want to target. You must also be aware where your product stands in the eyes and minds of the general population.

The main issue with targeting a broad range of audience is that your offer may not reach the intended group of people who have the highest purchasing capability due to a limited ad budget. In a sample ad we looked at, the Facebook campaign reached a total of 234,000 people, but the potential size of the audience for all ad groups went over 1.1 million people. What this means is that more than 850,000 people did not see the ad at all because of budget restraints.

How to Tell When your Ad Audience is too Broad?

Your audience size: Ask yourself if the millions of people that reached your ad are really interested in buying your product. If you think the answer is no, it is time to rethink and narrow down your audience to a niche demographic.

Ad reach: This is another way to see if your audience size is too big versus Facebook's projected ad reach and its total audience size. If the campaign shows the budget is for $1,000, then you can reach 150,000 people out of 1 million. You may need to downsize your audience then.

Broad demographics: If you notice that your audience reach is too broad, you can tweak this by excluding certain demographics through using behaviors or interests or even age range and gender.

4. Not Leveraging Custom Audiences

Another big mistake most marketers do is not leveraging their customized audiences. But this is the best way to win with Facebook Ads! Using Facebook custom audiences enables you to reach a target audience that is looking for your products and has the purchasing power as well as the split-second decision-making requirement. Get on Facebook Custom Audiences now to tap into this advertising potential.

How to leverage Facebook Custom Audiences:

Create campaigns to collect leads: You can target previous blog readers and give them an exclusive gift in exchange for their email address. By doing this to a small but committed group of people that is familiar with your brand, they will be much more willing to share their contact details with your business. For this, you need to use the new feature on Facebook called Facebook Leads ads campaign to collect all this information for high-value content of your users.

Remarket to past purchasers: You can also set up Custom Audience based on people who have previously visited your checkout pages or thank you's. This audience can be used for retargeting campaigns for upselling.

5. Not Excluding Past Converters

Most people, when they start out with Facebook advertising, end up making the mistake of forgetting to exclude the audience that

has already clicked on an ad and have been converted into a customer. Not excluding past converters may not be an ideal situation because:
- You end up wasting your valuable ad budget resources
- Your ads are not relevant to the people who have been converted.
- The more these people see your ads, the more they'll end up getting annoyed.
- The same people will see your ads over and over again and might suffer from ad fatigue or audience decay.

Facebook Ad Fatigue refers to the same people seeing your ad multiple times a day and their engagement with the ad will likely drop, and that means a higher cost to you, the advertiser.

Facebook Audience Decay refers to you, the advertiser, targeting the same group of people over a time period and diminishing their interest in you simply because they are annoyed with you.

To ensure you exclude these past converters from your Facebook audience, all you need to do is ensure you create a new Custom Audience for the people who have visited your web pages before. Use the "Exclude" feature located in the Audience tab on Facebook when you set up your ad campaign. You can remove the people who have already been to your page at some point.

6. Using the Wrong Ad Type

Using the wrong ad type is one of the most common mistakes. The great thing about Facebook is that advertisers have the freedom to experiment with different types of ads. While the newsfeed ads are one of the easiest and quickest ways to create an ad, that does not mean you should overlook other options such as Video Ads and Leads Ads.

For a quick overview, here are the types of ads on Facebook

you can use:
- Newsfeed Ad.
- Right Column Ad.
- Lead Ads.
- Carousel Ads.
- Dynamic Product Ads / DPA.
- Page Like Ads.
- Canvas Ads.
- Event Ads.
- Mobile App Install Ads.
- GIF Ads.

7. Ads That Fail to Draw Attention

The goal of advertisers is, of course, to create ads that attract. If a niche audience is what you are focusing on, then you need a brilliant ad message that is highly relevant to your target audience. In this day and age, the first thing people look at is images, and then they look at the headline. If your image AND your headline fail to attract the attention of your customers, then the likelihood of them skipping the ad is extremely high.

An ad that fails to attract your audience may be making these mistakes:
- It contains bad photography or low-resolution imaging.
- It does not employ the effective use of colors.
- It contains too many confusing elements that do not match your offer.

Ad research shows that people usually make up their minds within 90 seconds of seeing an ad, and that's a really small window. Research also states that about 63 to 90% of users base their assessment on the colors used on an ad. Adding colorful elements that match your brand will help people notice your ad and also equate it to your brand recognition.

8. Too Much Text on the Ad Image

Back when Facebook got into advertising, the rule was to have only 20% of text, otherwise Facebook could reject your ad. Now, Facebook is not as strict with this ruling, however, your ad ends up fitting into these four categories where Facebook basically rates your ad:
- Okay
- Low
- Medium
- High

You can use various tools like the Text Overlay Tool to test to see if you have too much text.

An ad with high-text density does not mean that Facebook is not going to deliver. However, this really means that you would have a smaller audience that will interact with your ads. Before your ad goes up, Facebook usually notifies you if your ad is text-heavy.

Keep your text density low if you do not want your ad results compromised. You can put in as much text as part of the caption.

9. Headlines without the Right Hook

A study conducted at Columbia University found that 59% of people never read anything more than the headline of your Facebook post before they decide to like it or share it. If you take this information into account, we are usually surrounded by 5,000 ads and branded messages on a daily basis. We are literally immune to ads. Additionally, with today's fast-paced lifestyle, our attention span is quite short. If your headline on your Facebook post fails to catch attention, then people will not read the copy of the ad.

How to write better headlines for your Facebook ads?

- Emphasize the benefits—One of the first things you should do is communicate your product's benefit, and if you can do this in 5 words or less, great! They will be more interested in what you have to offer and want to learn more by reading the copy.
- Keep your ad headlines short and clear—A short post with a 40 character limit was shown to be 86% more effective and received higher engagement than posts with more than 40 characters of words.
- Use numbers in headlines—Numbers attract, and if you use data such as statistics, you are 36% more capable of getting people to click on your ads.

10. Careless Copywriting

Did you know that you can write custom copy for each part of your ad when you create a Facebook ad campaign? A wrong line of text could potentially be the downfall of your ad and push away a reader.

Taking the time to craft high-quality ad copy will take your ad farther. You can also analyze the effectiveness of your campaign by running a split test and experiment with various ad copies.

How to write good Facebook ad copy:
- Begin by defining your goal for your ad. What is your ad campaign goal? To get people to buy something? To collect new leads? To create brand awareness? Each of the sentences you put in your ad should point towards your goal and nudge the audience to do what the ad says.
- Find the right tone of voice.
- Stick to what's important.
- Write with the customer in mind.

Testimonials are also a great way to write an ad copy. Research conducted by Econsultancy says that a website using customer reviews often get, at least, an increase of 63% of visitors who end up buying something.

Avoid putting in any cryptic or vague copy as people might not understand what you are trying to say. Keep your copy trustworthy, informative, and clear.

11. Missing a Clear Value Offer

Value offer is literally your goals translated into a focal point that you know will entice your customers. If the goal of your advertisement is to represent the key actions that your audience would most likely need to make, then the value offer should explain why they should take those specific steps.

You should also make sure your UVP (Unique Value Proposition) is clear, and it describes your product's benefit while differentiating you from the competition.

Essentially, you want to follow these rules for positioning your UVP: Your UVP should be in the customer's language. Do not let them guess.

- UVPs should be clear and easy to comprehend.
- UVP should be different and better than the competitors.
- Avoid hype words. People don't buy that anymore.
- UVP should be easy to read and understood in 5 seconds or less.

If you have these things down, you are in for a stellar ad! You should also remember to place your UVP in the headline, or front and center of your ad's image as this is the most visible location. Your ad message is delivered at first sight.

12. Stuffing Ads with Too Much Text

When it comes to Facebook ads, less is often more. The fewer distractions you have on your ad copy, the better since it gets your message across and helps people convert easily. On average, Facebook page posts usually are in the region of 157.7 characters, while user posts generate 121.5 characters and mobile posts, even less with 104.9 characters. Posts which a character range of 140 to 159 are usually 13.3% less engaging, on average, compared to posts with 120 to 139 characters.

One of the reasons why shorter Facebook posts work is because they are more concise, and they deliver the UVP message quickly. If you are creating a blog article, then a longer introductory ad will definitely make more sense.

13. Forgetting to Caption Video Ads

We tend to forget certain things about human nature. It is the same with Facebook video ads. Oftentimes, we forget that we need to add captions for the video, because by default videos are muted in the newsfeed. Facebook says that captioned video ads increase viewership by 12% on average. In another study, it showed that 41% of videos were completely ineffective without sound.

The chances of people not clicking "play" if you do not caption your video ads are high. This is due to the fact that they will not be able to see your ad or know what it is about.

Here are other things you want to avoid with video ad engagements:
- Not including an intro.
- Putting logos or credits at the beginning of the video.
- Attempting to put too much information in a single video.
- Using a person to speak on camera without sufficient context.

Making a video can take several days or, at the very least, several hours. Having a storyboard and thinking it through before starting the project is a best practice.

14. Bad Choice of Ad Placement

Score marketers found that desktop Facebook ads have a higher cost-per-click of 534% more than ads placed on an audience network + mobile. Desktop ads also perform much better in conversions. The ad placement plays a crucial role in the results of an ad. Facebook's ad placements include:
- Facebook newsfeeds (mobile and desktop).
- Right-hand column Facebook.
- Instagram.
- Audience Network.
- Instant Articles.
- In-stream Video.

Another reason why marketers make the mistake in choosing ad placements is the offer as well as the placement mismatch. For instance, if your goal is to create free trials for your software, Instagram ads may not be the best option because people are less likely to deal with businesses when they browse images of their friends.

One good way to find out if the ad placement brings in high returns on your investment is to do multiple ad placements and then analyze the results.

You can break down reports using Facebook Ads Manager and analyze which ads have lower cost-per-click and the highest conversion rate.

In case you are not sure which ad placements you should begin with, here are some suggestions:
- Conversions: Facebook and Audience Network.
- Brand awareness: Facebook and Instagram.

- Video views: Facebook, Instagram, and Audience Network.
- App installs: Facebook, Instagram, and Audience Network.
- Traffic (for website clicks and app engagement): Facebook and Audience Network
- Product catalog sales: Facebook and Audience Network.
- Engagement: Facebook and Instagram.

15. The 24/7 Ad Delivery

Having your ads run on a schedule makes more sense than having it run all day, all night. Here are some reasons why running ads all the time does not make sense:

- Audiences get tired of seeing your ad more quickly
- Your budget is spent on low-traffic hours when the conversion is very little.

To prevent ad fatigue and to ensure that you have your ad frequency under control, you can set up a custom schedule and promote your ads for a specific duration and time during the entire week. If you are worried that Facebook might end up delivering your ads to the same audience too many times per day, then you can also cap this using the Daily Unique Reach.

16. Amateur Ad Bidding

When it comes to ads, Facebook functions on an auction-type bidding feature the same way Google AdWords works. This is called PPC bidding, and it works extremely well when the stage is set just right. You can view and customize your bidding through Facebook Ads Manager using the "Budget and Schedule" tab.

Facebook ads have four different bidding options:

- *Conversions*–Your ads will be delivered as optimally as possible by Facebook to people who are most likely to convert. This method is a great area to start as Facebook optimizes the ad for you.
- *Link Clicks*–Facebook's primary goal is getting users to click on your ad and to follow the link or whichever goal you determine, whether it's to go to your websites landing page or view your Facebook profile.
- *Impressions*–Your ad is optimized with the main objective of increasing visibility to as many people as possible. This is a good option for businesses looking to build and strengthen brand awareness or sharing highly engaging content.
- *Daily Unique Reach*–Facebook optimizes increasing the visibility of your ads to people once a day. This is an excellent retargeting method to ensure that people will see your ads at least once every day and may not get tired or annoyed quickly.

There are three elements that determine your ad cost. These are: your ad relevance; your bid; and action rates, determined by Facebook algorithms. There is no right or wrong bidding method for any particular ad type. You just find the best bidding methods based on what's good and what works for your brand.

17. Slow Campaign Take-Off

A slow campaign take-off could be due to many reasons, some of them could be:
- There are just too many ad groups with A/B test variations with low budgets.
- The images used in the ad are not good enough to attract people's attention.
- The low relevance of ads due to poor audience targeting.
- Using the wrong bidding options.
- Being impatient and making unnecessary changes.
- Too much text.

So, what is the solution?

When starting a new campaign, you can assign Lifetime budgets that cross your planned budget. You are looking at about 10,000 impressions to check which ads work and which don't.

Use Facebook as a resource for the start of the campaign. For example, hit your campaign running with a budget of $1,500 instead of the planned $300, just to get the ball rolling.

18. Leaving Facebook No Time for Optimization

Another common rookie mistake with Facebook ads is to rely too much on immediate gratification and expecting Facebook to deliver astounding results in just a few hours. Don't write off a campaign as a failure if just after 3 hours, you don't see results. Usually, it takes about 24 hours for Facebook to optimize campaigns and a full 48 hours to reach a potential audience and bring in the results you want. Each time you make substantial changes to your campaign, wait

24 to 48 hours to expect any results or draw any conclusions.

19. Guessing, Not Testing

Another rookie mistake is not testing your ads but only guessing which works best. One of the best things you can do for the effort you put into creating your ads is running an A/B test to see which image ad performs best.

Doing a test enables you to have different options for images and ads rather than just relying on one. When you are not sure of your target audience or which ad copy to use or even what ad image works best, always experiment with the options you have.

20. Doing the Wrong Kind of A/B Tests

While testing is essential, conducting the wrong test is also a waste of time. Not every split testing you do is a brilliant idea. Your A/B testing is restricted to just a few tests a month on average due to limited ad budgets. A program called Optimizely has crafted a chart to assist experienced and less experienced A/B testers to prioritize tests efficiently.

A/B test elements that provide the biggest results:
- Countries.
- Precise interests.
- Mobile OS.
- Age ranges.
- Genders.
- Ad images.
- Titles.
- Relationship status.

- Landing page.
- Interested in.

There are plenty of different elements that connect to your target audience, which tell you how extremely important it is to figure out who to target, how often, how much, and so on.

21. Testing Too Many Things at Once

Sometimes, it is also easy for marketers and advertisers to get caught up in using different A/B testing simply because we want to see results in different situations. Plenty of people take research from step one and collect and lump all their interests into a huge list on Facebook Ad Manager, hoping to reach a large segment of the market. This is no doubt a bad practice as it will cost marketers much more money than their expenditure in the ad. You will get results, but you will not know which audience interest brought in the appropriate results.

This is like putting all your eggs in one basket and hoping for the biggest and best results.

For every experiment that you run, you will need to make sure that there is enough data for the testing results to show clear, valid, and statistically significant data. You should aim to collect at least 500 conversions before any conclusions are drawn. If there are two variations tested, then you need more ad impressions as well as conversions to pinpoint on a winning formula.

22. Low Landing Page and Facebook Ad Match

Imagine clicking on an ad for bar soap but being directed to a site where they sell portable chargers. That would be confusing and will only make the user have less trust towards the brand. Unfortunately, some marketers do not see this as a problem, and that's why users see plenty of Facebook ads that lead to irrelevant pages.

Promising one thing but delivering another thing, plus failing to retain a consistent message throughout your sales channel, is a costly and grave mistake.

When a user is interested in a specific product and clicks on an ad only to land on a different landing page, they will feel misled, lose interest, and leave the page. To maintain your landing page's value propositions and to keep your Facebook ad aligned, you must use the same key messages that are consistent throughout your sales funnel.

You should also avoid targeting all kinds of potential users in one go. Address your audience by segmenting them and connecting them with niche ad campaigns.

23. Poor Landing Page UX

Certain mistakes on your website's landing page will make you lose conversions. Even if your Facebook ad is amazing, landing page issues could compromise the effectiveness of your Facebook ads. Where Facebook ads are concerned, you should remember ad placements when you construct your landing page.

For example, if the mobile audience is what you are targeting, then make sure your landing page is optimized for mobile users and not desktop users. Crafting responsive designs to suit mobile users or desktop users should correlate with what your brand is giving as well as where your users usually hang-out. That said, almost 80% of users access websites through mobile anyway, and that's where most revenue also comes from. It is now more important to keep your landing page mobile optimized than ever before.

24. Neglecting the Conversion Tracking

It is extremely tempting to do conversion tracking and get your Facebook campaigns up and running. However, not tracking your conversions is not a sustainable route. Not conducting tracking means that you are doing your ads blindly. There is no way to analyze your ad results.

While you can see rudimentary trackings such as click-through rates and other metrics without doing any tracking adjustments, you do not have tracking for off-site conversions. Facebook can track off-platform conversions using Facebook Pixel. You just need to make sure to install it on your website.

To set up the basic Facebook Pixel code, follow these guidelines:

1. Go to the Pixels Page in Ads Manager.

2. Click Actions > View Code.

Each Facebook Ad Manager account can only have a one-pixel code. Use this pixel code on each page of your website.

3. Copy the code and paste it between the <head> tags on each web page, or in your website template to install it on your entire website. You can also use **Google Tag Manager**. To track specific conversions such as lead conversions or even purchases, you need to add a conversion tracking code. What's great is that you can track nine different specific events with Facebook Pixel:

This is a must-have in tracking your Facebook ad conversion, especially if you want to discover new advertising possibilities as well as establish successful A/B testing.

25. Losing Sight of the Real Goal

Each time you log into Facebook ads, be wary of vanity metrics such as your click-through rates and your cost-per-clicks. None of that matters if that data does not contribute to the ultimate goal you've established; whether that is increasing sales, increasing website visits, or increasing brand awareness or anything else. While the vanity metrics are great to look at, do not lose sight of your main goals when you analyze your campaign results.

26. Leaving Ads Unattended

Ads need to be tweaked, reviewed, and edited if necessary. Treat them like pets. Once you leave them alone, your ads could behave badly. AdEspresso had a first-hand lesson on this issue. They set up incredibly well-crafted and well-performing ad campaigns and left the campaigns to run for several months.

During that five month period, the cost-per-conversion on average for their campaigns increased by 1050%, going from $3.33 to $38.47. They threw in plenty of money but reached a relatively small audience and were saturated in just two months. To ensure that your Facebook ad campaigns remain under control, you must check up on them weekly. You will be better off reviewing ad campaigns more often than not once you have done the initial setup.

Here are the eight Facebook Ad metrics you need to keep track of:
- Ad frequency.
- Relevance score.
- Click-through-rate vs. conversion rate.
- Number of leads.
- Facebook Ads customer churn.
- Ad performance by placement.
- Clicks by interests.
- Ad engagement rate.

27. Neglecting the Ad Frequency

Ad frequency shows you how many times a person has seen

your ad on an average basis. The higher your ad frequency, the higher the likelihood that people will become tired and bored seeing your ad multiple times. AdEspresso also analyzed how frequency affects the click-through rate, cost-per-click, and cost-per-conversion of ad campaigns. Here are their findings:

Frequency	CTR Decrease	CPC Increase
1	0	0
2	-8.91%	+49.82%
3	-16.92%	+62.20%
4	-23.34%	+68.02%
5	-29.72%	+98.51%
6	-41.19%	+127.32%
7	-41.38%	+127.26%
8	-48.97%	+138.31%
9	-49.87%	+161.15%

Source: https://adespresso.com/blog/facebook-ads-frequency/

The click-through-rate decreased as much as 8.91% when the same people saw the ad twice. However, when shown repetitive ads for 5 consecutive times, the cost-per-click increased to 98.51% higher compared to the first ad delivery.

The general rule is to keep your ad frequency to 3-5 points, unless your ad is really entertaining and has become viral.

Remarketing of Facebook campaigns have shown better results even when the ad frequency was over 10 ad views. Never make the rookie mistake of neglecting ad frequencies that are high since you can use it as an indicator your campaigns may need updated.

28. *Not Using Auto-Optimization*

If you are worried about high ad frequency and decreasing

campaign results, and you're also spending too much time checking your ad reports on Facebook, you can efficiently tackle this task through Facebook Automated Rules. This feature enables marketers to keep ad campaigns under control.

It also allows four things to take place automatically. You can:
- Turn off (campaign, ad set or ad).
- Send notification to the ad manager (you).
- Adjust budget (increase/decrease daily/lifetime budget by...).
- Adjust manual bid (increase/decrease bid by...).

These rules can be applied to any specific campaign, ad sets, and ads that you have selected. You can also use it on active campaigns.

The current conditions you can set are:
- Cost per Result.
- Cost per Add Payment Info (Facebook Pixel).
- Cost per Click (Link).
- Cost per App Install.
- Cost per Add to Cart (Facebook Pixel).
- Cost per Initiate Checkout (Facebook Pixel).
- Cost per Purchase (Facebook Pixel).
- Cost per Lead (Facebook Pixel).
- Cost per Complete Registration (Facebook Pixel).
- CPM (Cost per 1,000 impressions).
- Daily Spent.
- Frequency.
- Impressions.
- Lifetime Spent.
- Reach.
- Results.

If you want to create a new ad rule, all you do is select one or various campaigns or ads, and then click on Create Rule.

Once you have selected the campaign or ad, you can then create custom combinations or specific conditions that may trigger specific actions.

For instance, you can check to see if Facebook can automatically turn off active ads in your campaign with an ad frequency of more than 4.

This automated rule feature does a good job of notifying a marketer when a campaign begins to garner lower results, and it also helps to keep ad costs under control.

29. Missing Out on the Conclusions

There are some marketers who have run multiple Facebook ad campaigns but always end up making the same mistakes. You can avoid this by keeping a log of your ad campaigns or tracking the results in an excel spreadsheet.

In a spreadsheet you can note key achievements, takeaways, and any mistakes you've made for each Facebook campaign.

Take a few minutes to conclude what you have done in your previous Facebook campaign before you trash it; take note of what worked and what went wrong. It is always a good idea to double down on what works.

Chapter 7: Understanding Facebook Advertising

To understand Facebook advertising is to know what Facebook Business Manager is. The Facebook Business Manager tool is designed for managing your Facebook pages and ad accounts.

When you use this, you will be able to:
- Manage your Facebook page admins and ad accounts.
- see who has access to your pages and ad accounts.
- remove or change admin permissions.
- work with agencies and also share your business account with agencies, so they can manage your ad campaigns via Facebook.
- Manage multiple ad accounts as well as users all under the Business Manager account.

Essentially, there are two main roles in the Facebook Business Manager, which are the Admin and Employee.

Each of these roles have different access levels. There is also a different tool for Facebook ad accounts that enables the admin to manage and edit in the business account itself.

To start advertising on Facebook, you will be required to have a Business Manager account that enables you to manage at least one Facebook Page.

To add an advertising account to your Business Manager:
- Open your Business Manager Settings.
- Under the tab People and Assets, click on "Ad Accounts."
- On the right side of the page, select "Add New Ad Accounts."

- Choose one of the 3 options: "Claim Ad Account," "Request Access to an Ad Account," or "Create a New Ad Account."

You also need to add a credit card to the account and provide other essential information before advertising.

Setting Up Your Ad Account Info

Facebook will not allow you to start spending unless there is a value payment connected and some relevant business information shared. To set up your account, click on "Ad Account Settings" on your Business Manager.

Fill in the necessary information for your business, such as the address.

Billing details can be added under the "Payments" tab by clicking on "Add Payment Method." Some localities request VAT numbers. You can also choose the currency you want to deal with and your specific time zone. Once you have filled in your account information, click on "Save Changes." You can then proceed to the "Billing & Payment Methods" page.

Setting Up Your Billing & Payment Information

Adding credit card details should be done under "Billing & Payment Methods" in the Business Manager menu.

At the Billing section, you can do the following:
- Insert new payment methods.
- Edit your existing payment methods.
- Set the spending limit for your account.

If you would like to add a new payment method:
- Click on "Add Payment Method."

- Choose the method you want to add.
- Fill in the specific information.
- Click on "Continue."

Multiple payment types are accepted by Facebook; the major ones being credit cards and PayPal payments.

As you begin adding more advertising content, it would be good practice to add a secondary payment option. Should your primary card expire or if you reach your monthly limit, or worse it is blocked for some reason, your campaigns can still run with a secondary payment option. If Facebook does not have enough funds, your campaigns could be paused until you top up the necessary funds, and you could end up having to restart them one by one manually. Facebook will automatically bill your secondary credit card when your primary card is unavailable. This keeps things running smoothly.

Editing Your Payment Options

Should you want to make changes to your Facebook advertising payments, you can do it via the same page by clicking on "Edit Payment Methods."

You will not be able to delete your primary source of payment unless you add another payment method. Only then can you delete your primary option. This works for most payment options on the net.

How and when are you billed? Billing is often done on two occasions:

- At the end of every month.
- When you reach your billing limit.

Billing limit or threshold is what you will be billed on your primary payment method each time you reach a limit. The amount of this limit is based on your billing history, and it usually varies.

When you first start advertising, this threshold is usually low at around $25. Each time you spend $25, you will be billed for that same amount. However, as you continue spending and your payments are processed correctly, your threshold is automatically increased to anywhere from $50, $250, $500, and finally, $750.

These limits don't have any immediate impact on your advertising campaigns. They just affect how often you will be charged.

Dealing with fewer invoices is the advantage to having a higher threshold.

You can always contact Facebook should you have any issues with billing or if you want to change your threshold.

Setting up the Account Spending Limit

You can cap your account spending if you do not want your ad campaigns to exceed your advertising budget. This is also important when you have given agencies access to your ad manager account and want to only spend what has been budgeted.

Setting the limit is very simple. Just click the "Set Account Spending Limit" and set the amount. Do not set it too low or you will end up updating your limit often. Each time your limit is reached, your account(s) will be paused for at least 15 minutes. It should also be noted: your account spending limit does not have an impact on your ad's delivery pace.

Facebook Ad Account Limits

Limits, unfortunately, exist in Facebook Ads but these limits are not a hindrance to your campaigns. While it's not bothersome, it is still good to know what these limits are.

Here are the limits of Facebook Power Editor:

- Users can manage up to a maximum of 25 ad accounts.

- Each ad account can contain up to 25 users.

- An average ad account contains approximately 5,000 ads and 1,000 ad sets.

These limits apply to ads and campaigns that have not been deleted. Even when you reach your limit, you can always delete older

campaigns and their ads.
Review Your Notification Settings

Obviously, you will want to stay informed regarding any updates occurring on your ad account. Make sure you turn on your Facebook Notifications, so you know what is happening with your campaigns. Sometimes, they can flood your inbox.

You may want to do one of two things:

1. Change the frequency of the email notifications.

2. Separate your email from Facebook so it goes into a different tab or folder and not in your primary inbox.

To edit your notification settings:

- Click on the settings tab on the Ad Account Page.

- Click on "Notifications" from the menu on the left.

- You can add or remove notifications, based on what you want to be notified about.

- You can set up notifications, so you receive the most important ones.

Review Your Ad Account Roles

If adding new user admins is what you want to do with your Facebook advertising account, then click on "Account Roles."

In this section, you can add new admins or edit permissions for existing users.

Once you are done with this, you have set up your account management, and you are all set!

Traffic and Leads for Your Website

The most common use for Facebook Ads is to drive traffic to a specific website and also to create brand awareness. Directing users to your site can increase the website's overall reach, get users to buy your product, sign up for your service, or subscribe to your newsletter.

Various types of ads and how you can use them to drive traffic to your site:

Link Click Ads

Supported placements:

- Column Desktop.
- Newsfeed Mobile.
- Newsfeed Audience.
- Network Instagram.

Specs:

- Recommended image size: 1,200 x 628 pixels.
- Ad copy text: 90 characters.
- Headline: 25 characters.
- Link Description: 30 characters.

When you think Facebook ads, the first thing that might come to mind is Link Click Ads. This ad serves to promote external websites and also send users to a specific landing page or even a specific blog post. Link Click Ads can be used with several placements, which enables marketers to provide the same ad across various newsfeeds and effectively reach a large audience. This type of ad performs exceptionally well and can also generate likes for your page, but don't forget to check the comments you receive and reply to them because this contributes to the ad's performance and engagement.

Video Ads

Supported placements:
- Newsfeed Mobile.
- Newsfeed Audience.
- Network Instagram.

This is another form of Link Click Ads, but instead of a stationary image, you use a video.

Specs:
- Ad copy text: 90 characters.
- Aspect ratios supported: 16:9 to 9:16.
- File size: up to 4 GB max.
- Continuous looping available.
- Video can be as long as 120 minutes, but most top-performing videos are 15-30 seconds.

Boosted Page Posts

Supported placements:
- Newsfeed Mobile.
- Newsfeed Audience.
- Network Instagram.

Each time you post on your page, Facebook gives you a chance to boost your post. You will see a conveniently located button at the bottom right corner of a post. When you click on it, you can set the post to target a specific audience, add in your bidding methods, as well as promote your page's post to more people on Facebook.

Specs:
- Recommended image size: 1,200 x 628 pixels.
- Ad copy text: unlimited.
- Headline: 25 characters.
- Link Description: 30 characters.

The Boosted Page Post will look exactly like any other Facebook post, except "Sponsored" will appear at the top of the ad.

Multi-Product (Carousel Ads)

Supported placements:
- Newsfeed Mobile.
- Newsfeed Audience.
- Network Instagram.

This carousel format allows the advertiser to add up to 10 items, which could be a combination of videos and images and even links to a single ad unit.

For e-commerce advertisers looking to promote a variety of products from their store, this is an extremely convenient and useful feature.

This feature really works great even for marketers wanting to promote different types of posts and offers, and it attracts audiences to view a variety of content based on the brand or product.

Specs:
- Recommended image size: 1080 x 1080 or 600 x 600 pixels.
- Ad copy text: 90 characters.
- Headline: 25 characters.

- Link Description: 30 characters.

Dynamic Product Ads (DPA)

Supported placements:
- Newsfeed Mobile.
- Newsfeed Right Column.
- Audience Network.
- Instagram.

These dynamic product ads that Facebook has introduced are like remarketing display ads on speed. These ads target users based on previous actions whether on your website or application with an ad that is perfectly timed.

To use this feature, all you need to do is upload your product catalog and double check that your Facebook pixel is installed on all your site pages. This means Facebook handles the retargeting and automation for you.

Specs:
- Recommended image size: 1,200 x 628 pixels or 600 x 600 pixels.
- Ad copy text: 90 characters.
- Headline: 25 characters.
- Link Description: 30 characters.

Facebook Lead Ads

Supported placements:

- Newsfeed Mobile.
- Newsfeed Audience.
- Network Instagram.

Lead Ads are one of the best ways to get leads. This type of ad allows users to download your content or sign up for an offer without ever leaving Facebook's platform. Lead Ads are perfect for attaining potential customers email address.

Specs:

- Recommended image size: 1,200 x 628 pixels.
- Ad copy text: 90 characters.
- Headline: 25 characters.
- Link Description: 30 characters.

Context card can be in paragraph format, which has no character limit, or 5-bullet point format, which allows for 80 characters per bullet.

- Context card headline: 60 characters.
- Context card button: 30 characters.
- Privacy Policy and website URL links are required.

The moment someone has filled in the form, Facebook ad accounts stores the email address. Among the easiest ways to transfer new leads from Facebook to your CRM system is to automate the whole process. This is one extra thing you can do when setting up as campaigns via Facebook.

Canvas Ads

Supported placements:
- Mobile Newsfeed.

Canvas by Facebook is completely interactive and allows users to engage with your brand on Facebook; it is only available on mobile version as it was built for mobile usage. Using Canvas enables your audience to swipe through a carousel of images, and even tilt it in different directions. You can zoom in and zoom out using your fingertips. Canvas loads much faster than average mobile web apps.

Specs:
- Recommended image size: 1,200 x 628 pixels.
- Ad copy text: 90 characters.
- Headline: 45 characters.

Canvas has the following possible components:
- Header with logo.
- Full-screen image.
- Text block.
- Button for offsite links.
- Image carousel.
- Auto-play video.
- Full-screen tilt-to-pan image.
- Product set.

Collection Ads

Supported placements:
- Mobile Newsfeed.

With Collection Ads, you can showcase several products sold on your site on Facebook. This new format enables people to discover your brand, browse your products, and purchase your products in a highly visual and immersive channel.

Specs:
- Image Size: 1,200 x 628 pixels recommended.
- Image Ratio: 1.9:1.
- Headline: 25 characters recommended

Like & Engagement for Your Page

The type of ad you choose on Facebook depends entirely on the campaign outcome you are looking for. Two particular campaign objectives help to increase the number of likes on your Facebook page as well as increase the reach of your content posted. With recent updates to Facebook, your regular posts on your page will reach an organic audience of 2-3%. Using Facebook ads is a great way to let all your fans and potential fans see your messages.

Page Like Ads

Supported placements:
- Column Desktop.
- Newsfeed Mobile.
- Newsfeed.

Page Like Ads are the most commonly used ads to increase page Likes. These ads can be displayed on a variety of placements and also include a visible call-to-action for users to like your page immediately. When you advertise for likes, keep in mind that it's not about getting any random person to like your page. It is about choosing the right audience interested in your page and the content it offers. To achieve increased likes, it is important to pick the right image, so you maximize the performance of Facebook ads and improve reach.

Page Post Photo Ads

Supported placements:
- Column Desktop.
- Newsfeed Mobile.
- Newsfeed.

When should you engage your page's fans? Using the page photo ads is the best time to feature beautiful images. Choose the right image, and set yourself up with comments, likes, and increased interaction. You can also insert specific links in your text description, so people can be directed to a page on your website.

Page Post Video Ads

Supported placements:
- Column Desktop.
- Newsfeed Mobile.
- Newsfeed.

One of the highest engagement procurers is Video Advertising. It creates a strong connection between brand and user, and almost any company can make simple videos to connect with their audience and speak to them in the way images cannot.

Video ads also have the ability to retarget a certain segment of visitors based on how much of the video they have watched. Because of this, video ads are perfect for retargeting especially with other types of ads.

Specs:

- Ad copy text: 90 characters.

- Aspect Ratios Supported: 16:9 (full landscape) to 9:16 (full portrait).

- File size: up to 4 GB max.

- Video can be as long as 120 minutes, but most top-performing videos are 15-30 seconds.

- Audio: Stereo AAC audio compression, 128kbps + preferred.

Page Post Text

Supported placements:

- Column Desktop.

- Newsfeed Mobile.

- Newsfeed.

This ad format is focused on page engagement. Despite that, not many marketers use it when there is the photo option. In truth, pictures perform better for most audiences. Avoid this ad if you can unless you have a stellar tagline that will bring in the audience that you want.

Mobile and Desktop Apps Install

Facebook has become the biggest mobile advertiser since the launch of its mobile application. The App Install offers a distinctive opportunity to attract all mobile users on iOS and Android. These ad extensions are useful and should be taken into account if you are in the mobile app industry, especially since they are built for that specific purpose.

Mobile App

Supported placements:
- Mobile Newsfeed.

Using the Mobile App Ads is a perfect choice if you want to drive mobile app installations. Ads are displayed and optimized for the mobile version of Facebook's newsfeed. When users click on install as a call-to-action, they will be directed immediately to the App Store pop up. This definitely increases conversion rates. There will be plenty more targeting options when using Facebook's mobile ad format. For instance, when you choose the iOS/Android version, you are targeting users on tablets and mobile devices. You could also target only users connected to a Wi-Fi network.

Specs:
- Recommended image size: 1,200 x 628 pixels.
- Image ratio: 1.9:1.
- Ad copy text: Up to 90 characters.
- Your image may not include more than 20% text.

Desktop App

Supported placements:
- Column Desktop.
- Newsfeed.

Enables you to channel users to your Facebook wall and engage with it.

Specs:

- Recommended image size: 1,200 x 628 pixels.
- Image ratio: 1.9:1.
- Ad copy text: Up to 90 characters.

Instagram Mobile App Ads

Supported placements: Instagram

You can also advertise your mobile app via Instagram. This is perfect since Instagram is only useable on mobile, which means users who access your ad are interested in what you have to offer and are more likely to download your app. Both video ads and photo ads work in Instagram Mobile App Ads.

Specs:

- Image ratio: 1:1.
- Image size: 1080 x 1080 pixels.
- Minimum resolution: 600 x 315 pixels / 600 x 600 pixels / 600 x 750 pixels.
- Maximum resolution: 1936 x 1936 pixels.
- Caption: Text only, 125 characters recommended.
- Visitors to Your Store or Event.

When targeted effectively, these ads perform very well.

Event Ads

Supported placements:
- Right Column.
- Desktop Newsfeed.
- Mobile Newsfeed.

Facebook Events, while not exactly a form of advertising, is an exceptional way to attract online attendees. Using Facebook events can dramatically boost your event coverage, especially when the right kind of targeting is used.

Based on the relevance and size of your event, limiting your geographical reach will help in attracting a niche living in the same region or city as the event.

Specs:
- Recommended image size: 1920×1080 pixels.
- Image ratio: 1.9:1.
- Ad copy text: Up to 90 characters.
- Headline: 25 characters.
- Link Description: 30 characters.
- Offer Claims.
- Supported placements: Right.
- Column Desktop.
- Newsfeed.
- Mobile Newsfeed.

This feature is ideal for any physical store owner who wants to attract people to their store, especially for sales or any seasonal promotion. Once your offer ad is live, an interested user who clicks on your ad and redeems the offer will subsequently receive an email containing the details and terms of use.

Specs:
- Recommended image size: 1,200 x 628 pixels.
- Image ratio: 1.9:1.
- Offer title: Up to 25 characters.
- Ad copy text: Up to 90 characters.

To be able to craft an offer, your page should have garnered at least 50 likes.

Local Awareness Ads

Supported placements:
- Column Desktop.
- Newsfeed.
- Mobile Newsfeed.

Using Local Awareness Ads is another excellent way to garner attention to your store. This ad type works well combined with Facebook's location-based targeting, helping you to reach people who are currently near your store. There are different call-to-actions which you can use such as "Call Now," and "Send Message." People can easily and conveniently contact or find you.

Specs:
- Recommended image size: 1,200 x 628 pixels.
- Image ratio: 1.9:1.
- Text: 90 characters.

- Headline: 25 characters.
- News Feed description: 30 characters.

Who are your customers?

Getting to know your customers is an integral part of successful Facebook ad campaigns. With over 1 billion active users daily, it is crucial that you target specific audiences truly interested in your product.

Advertising is getting the right customers and not about getting random clicks or likes. You want to choose the audience that sees the benefits of your product, but you should also keep testing your options to see which one works in what condition and what platform.

How to Create Facebook Audiences

You need to use this convenient Facebook tool called "Audience Manager Tool" to create niche audiences and manage these different categories. This tool is found in the Business Manager application at the Audiences Tab.

At this tab, you can see all the Facebook audiences you have created and saved. To understand targeting possibilities, let's look at the primary audience types that Facebook has:

- Saved Audiences.
- Custom Audiences.
- Lookalike Audiences.

These various types of audiences provide plenty of additional options for crafting the perfect target audience for your Facebook campaigns.

Facebook Saved Audiences

Saved audiences are the variety that can be defined by choosing people's age, gender, interests, income level, and even devices. Saved audiences can be created in the campaign setup phase or in the Audience Manager.

Location-based targeting

Facebook also allows you to target people in specific locations, including:
- Country.
- State/Region.
- Counties.
- DMA (Designated Market Area).
- City.
- Postal Code.
- Specific Address Radius.

All you need to do is type in the area or region you want to target.

Another layer of location targeting you can do to make it more specific is to locate using the last updated location of an actual Facebook user.
- People who live in this location–Location is determined by the location on a user's Facebook profile and confirmed by their IP address.
- People recently in this location–use data in the mobile device usage in the geographic area you intend to target.
- People traveling to this location–Users who keyed in a specific geographic area as a recent location that is, at least, 100 miles away from their home location.

Demographics-based targeting

When you click on the Demographics tab, you will find even more targeting topics to refine your audience based on many options.

The basic 3 are:
- Age–if you want to target audiences based on a specific age group, you can easily refine it by providing Facebook what your ideal customer's age range is.
- Gender–You can also target a particular gender that would appeal to your brand
- Language–Target the people who can understand your ads in a specific language.

There are more refined categories if you want to be more specific, such as political views, life events, job titles, ethnicity, and so on.

Interest-based targeting

The best and easiest Facebook ad targeting options is "Interests" because they allow you to pinpoint on people specifically interested in a subject related to your product. You could target people interested in your competitor or your broader market segment, or even specific magazines and blogs related to your industry.

To create targeting based on interests, you can simply type in one interest or browse the selection with hundreds of interests, and Facebook will suggest other related topics.

These interests are calculated on a user's behavior on Facebook, their likes and interests, apps they have engaged in, pages they have liked, and more. Adding more than one interest will specifically target people with, at least, one of them, which will make your reach broader.

Behavior-based targeting

Behaviors are different from "Interests" in a way that it is focused on the user's purchasing history, events they like, personal anniversaries, etc. This data is collected by Facebook by analyzing various data sets; external and internal. While they are not always mandatory, they work great for targeting people who have recently purchased something; such as planning a holiday or preparing for one.

This information can be extremely useful if you are in the hotel industry or traveling industry. It is worth checking to see if they can work for your business.

Facebook Custom Audiences

These types of target audiences are perhaps your highest value as they enable you to retarget past website visitors as well as users who have previously engaged with your content. There are plenty of ways to create custom audiences.

Creating Custom Audiences from Customer Files

You can create your Facebook Custom Audience by checking your existing customer files and look at email accounts, phone numbers, location, and even app IDs. This information is helpful in targeting newsletter subscribers as well as app users.

Here are the steps to create a custom audience:
- Create a Facebook Custom Audience.
- Choose the "Customer File" option.
- Choose either to add a customer file or import contacts from MailChimp.
- Import your customer data to create a new Custom Audience.
- Select your identifiers.

- Upload a customer file.
- Give your Custom Audience a name.
- Customer files can include 15 different identifiers, the most popular ones being:
- Email.
- Phone number.
- Mobile advertiser ID.

Creating Custom Audiences Based on Website Traffic

Website traffic allows you to create re-marketing and retargeting campaigns for people who have previously engaged with your app or website. This traffic is always very high value as these users who are seeing your ad now have already shown a degree of interest in your product previously. If your website is built on a WordPress platform, you can create custom audiences using the Pixel Caffeine plugin.

You also need to have the Facebook Pixel installed. Next, just go to the Audience Manager and create your Custom Audience based on your previous website traffic history.

Here, you have multiple options of targeting to choose from:
- You can choose to target people who have visited your website.
- You can choose to target people who have visited specific websites related to your industry.
- You can choose people who have visited specific web pages.
- You can choose to target people who have not visited your website for a period of time.
- A combination of the choices above.

Creating Custom Audiences Based on App Activity

You can also reach out to users who have engaged with your app and set up a specific Facebook audience for those types of groups. To do this, you can target users based on their app activity, but first you also need to register your app and set it up in the app events. You can now target people who have made specific actions on your app and even target them based on a specific timeframe.

For instance, you can select an activity based on a purchasing event and specify, "In the Last 90 days" to reach people who have completed an in-app purchase event in the past 90 days.

Creating Custom Audiences Based on Engagement

Another way you can target specific users is to look at how they have engaged with your Facebook content such as the videos they have seen or the posts they have liked on your Page.

Custom Audiences has the capacity to focus on people who have conducted the following activity:
- Visited your Facebook Page.
- Engaged with your Facebook Page posts or ads.
- Clicked on any call-to-action buttons.
- Sent a message to your Page.
- Saved your Page or posts.

This targeting option enables you to reach a "high-potential" audience since they are most likely interested in learning about what you have to offer.

How to Narrow Down Your Audiences

Narrowing your audience is the same as niche targeting. You want to focus on users that have the highest potential of engagement and who make purchasing decision to purchase your product or service or attend your event or engage in your activity. It doesn't matter if you have a huge advertising budget. Targeting and narrowing down your audience ensures you meet the right ones without wasting your time.

You can narrow your audience pool with targeting options when you create your Saved Audiences, by adding or subtracting different targeting options based on your specific marketing needs. In doing so, your audience pool will either grow bigger or smaller. This will ultimately help you create niche audiences.

You can include or exclude your interests or demographics, so your ads reach the relevant people and not the same people over and over.

Facebook Ads Reporting & Optimization

When you are done setting up your Facebook Ad Campaign, whether it is your first or your twentieth, you still need to continue monitoring and reviewing your campaigns, even though Facebook does an excellent job auto-optimizing campaigns. Checking to see whether everything is running smoothly is important as it will help you see what works and also add in any new insights you have gained during your existing or upcoming ad campaigns. Also, no matter how amazing your campaign is, you always need to monitor its performance. No unattended campaign lasts forever even in the most ideal of situations.

When reviewing campaigns or monitoring its progress, always ask

yourself:
- Where can you see your Facebook campaign results?
- How else can you optimize your campaigns based on the current insights?

Facebook Ads Reporting in the Ads Manager

The Facebook Ad Manager is the easiest way to review your campaign performance. With the ad manager, you can filter your campaigns by dates, objectives, and zoom in on any campaign to see its performance based on its ad set.

You can also set the correct date range when looking for reports and compare different date ranges to see how your campaign has performed over time; you can select a date range of 7 days. Longer campaign periods could change your metrics making it a little difficult to understand and assess recent campaign performance.

As you look at the Campaigns tab in the Ads Manager, you will see the reporting table with different metrics such as:
- Cost-per-click.
- Cost-per-conversion.
- Impressions.
- Unique Link Clicks.

This is where you can get an overview of all your Facebook campaigns performance.

You can also select a specific campaign by clicking on the checkbox in front of the campaign name. Here, you can also navigate the Ad Sets and Ads tabs to view the performance of every individual campaign unit.

The awesome thing about this page is that Facebook automatically displays the most useful data for each campaign.

Managing Your Ad Report's Columns

While Facebook displays the most amazing ad metrics, generally you can still customize the ad reports according to your needs. You can do this by clicking the Columns menu to choose between different ad reports to change the metrics.

You can select pre-set reports or just create a new customer ad report by clicking on "Customize Columns."

Facebook Ads Manager allows you to see many different metrics. Here are the most important and insightful report metrics you can look into. The ad report metrics depends entirely on your goals and objectives; so of course, you can change it according to your needs.

- Performance: Results, Result Rate, Reach, Frequency, Impressions, Delivery, Social Reach, Social Impressions, People Taking Action, Positive & Negative Feedback, Amount Spent, etc.
- Engagement: Post Engagement, Post Comments, Post Shares, Page Engagement, Page Likes, Page Mentions, Event Responses, Check-Ins, Offer Claims, etc.
- Clicks: Link clicks, Unique Link Clicks, CTR, Social Clicks, etc.
- Messaging: New Messaging Conversations, Messaging Replies, Cost per New Messaging Conversation, etc.
- Media: Video Average Watch Time, Canvas View Time, 3-Second Video Views, 10-Second Video Views, 30-Second Video Views, Video Watches at 25%, Video Watches at 100%, etc.
- Website Conversions: Website Leads, Website Searches, Website Adds to Cart, Website Registrations Completed, Cost per Website Conversion, Cost per Website Purchase, Website Conversion Value, Website Custom Conversions, etc.

- Apps: Desktop App Installs, Mobile App Actions, Mobile App Adds to Cart, Mobile App Purchases, Cost per App Install, etc.
- On-Facebook: On-Facebook Purchases, Leads (Form), Cost per On-Facebook Purchase, etc.
- Offline: Offline Leads, Store Visits, Offline Purchases, Offline Ads to Cart, Cost per Offline Purchases, etc.

Once you have created the ad reports you need, don't forget to save them! You can also set any new report as the default option.
- Advanced reporting with Campaign Breakdown.
- Apart from the campaign metrics you can view on your Ad Manager reports, you can also take your reporting routine to a different level by using the Breakdown menu.
- With this feature, you can look at your metrics by using:
    - Delivery: age, gender, location, browsing platform, platform, device, time of day, etc.
    - Action: conversion device, destination, video view type, video sound, carousel card, etc.
    - Time: day, week, two weeks, month.

You can select different criteria from each of the sections above.

With the campaign breakdown, you can understand the goals of your campaign effectively and answer plenty of questions such as:

- The ad placements that works the best.
- The times of day or weekdays that deliver the most conversions at the lowest cost.
- The best-performing target countries.

To categorize your ad campaigns using the different criteria, you need to select one or more Facebook campaigns first. Next, select the criteria you want to focus on from the Breakdown option. Because Facebook Ads have plenty of reporting options, take your time to explore them. In time, you will gain a better understanding of the process and what ad metrics are important to look for your brand and optimization.

Save & Automate Campaign Reports

With Facebook campaign reports, you can also schedule daily or weekly reports to be delivered to your inbox, and all for free. When you are done crafting a report using Facebook Ads Manager, you can save the report and send to your inbox periodically.

All you need to do is click on "Report" located next to your account name.

Go to "Save new report..." and a small window prompt will appear where you can input the name of the report as well as set it up to be sent either daily, weekly, or monthly. Usually, a weekly report would suffice unless you want to track specific daily activities on your ad campaigns.

Chapter 8: Psychology of Facebook Ads

The psychology of Facebook Ads: what do people think when they look at your ad and what do people look for when they're on Facebook. Specifically, what is your audience looking for?

Content nowadays is driven visually. Consumers rarely buy anything without having a look at what they are purchasing. More often than not, people prefer trying it, touching it, holding, and smelling, and so on–basically using all their senses. With online retail, we cannot do much of touching and trying. It is usually a visual representation of a product.

Online images have come a long way. From the mediocre product photo or photos, e-commerce sites have evolved to enable a much deeper consumer experience to allow customers to understand the product they are purchasing–even without the need of touching or feeling it.

A good visual representation of a product will increase purchase rates, and that is why marketers need to work twice as hard to ensure their products come alive via excellent photography, display, graphics, and product description.

In a world where everything is becoming more and more visually driven (think Instagram and Pinterest), consumers can now take photos of a product and post it online. People take images of food, of the venue, of decorations, of buildings, and so on until we get a good idea of where the place is, and even the street it is on (Google StreetView) before even physically going there on their own.

Places like TripAdvisor allows both the management of a property as well as the patronizing customers to post pictures, and viewers can see what it is really like. Most people visiting the website often click on images taken by visitors instead of the management photos as it gives them an unpolished view of the place.

Instagram, being a visual app, has enabled people to build businesses just by posting images of their products and services on it. The more visually appealing an image, the more likes, the more reposts, and the more comments.

In this chapter, we will focus on images and what they can do to your online site, increasing your business, and increasing the conversion rate.

If you are selling a product or service, then you must have images of very high quality. In fact, any website in 2017 and beyond must have good quality design and pictures if they want to continue staying at the top of SEO rankings.

Too many websites attempt to sell their products with very low-quality images. This puts consumers off, and they wander to a competitor's website, who can offer a much better visual representation of their products.

1. Alternate & Detailed Views

You want to entice customers to purchase your product. Apart from a single photo, give users views from different angles as it can show character and carry a brand. A great example of thoughtful and visually appealing photography would be by Poplook, a clothing brand. The website gives you a default image of the product in full size and it also shows your clickable thumbnails of the product in different positions and angles. Check it out for yourself by going to Poplook.com

2. Context

Context matters when selling a product as it gives users an experience of using or wearing a product. You can show the product in its context. Following the example of Poplook, they also have a zoom in function and you can see the details of the clothing. There is also a short video of a model wearing the clothing item.

3. Avoid Unrelated Stock Photos

People pay attention to images. When websites were new, stock photos were regularly used to compliment content on a website. However, as websites keep evolving and users' tastes, interests, and levels of interest keep changing, people want to see more genuine content.

A website can create better authority in its field and increase traffic simply by using real people. Not models posing in stock photos but actual scenarios in their office space, road shows, venue, events, and so on. Purchasing stock photos will not do much nowadays. If you use stock photos of models in suits shaking hands or looking randomly into a computer, you are oblivious, and you think your customers are gullible. Genuine pictures showcasing the lifestyle of your company, your employees, the surrounding of your firm is one hundred times better than regular stock photos.

4. Focus Attention on Your Products

Did you know the eye focuses on a certain item when viewing an image? Tracking the eye movement of users when they view images on your website gives you an insight into human perception, which can be used in the design of your advertising, promotional, and marketing material.

This research conducted on eye tracking shows where men and women look and for how long, when viewing a product.

Even how products are placed in a supermarket can show how people look at items in a store or where their focus goes first.

These valuable insights can give you a good idea of how to design your online website and what images to place first in order to attract the user to buying your product or subscribing to your service.

5. Utilize Rotating Images

360-degree rotating images provides a user a whole new view of the product. This technology is a bit expensive, so it may be better suited to you if you are selling a high-end product such as cameras, laptops, vehicles, branded shoes, and so on, this 3D rotating feature will definitely boost your conversion rate. There are many design companies that offer this kind of specialization and there are also do-it-yourself built-in plugins and programs that enable you to do this on your own.

6. Product Images Located in Search Window Boost Conversions

Product images used in dropdown search results also give an extra boost for conversion rates. This increases the customer's likelihood of purchasing a product, because again you are using a visual aid to guide the customer in making a quicker decision of which product to purchase. It makes searching for products easier thus speeding up their time in making a decision. It also makes a customer feel like they have an increased sense of what they want based on what is available on your site.

Many companies have expressed their finding that using the product images in the site's dropdown search bar, we get a 100% lift in conversion rate among shoppers who use site search." Image-based search results have been shown to increase conversion rates and sales in online shopping and e-commerce sites.

7. Human photos on a Landing Page Increase Sales and Conversions

Adding a human face to landing pages increases conversion rates as well. People want to connect with a product or service and having a human face at the very beginning of their visit to your site makes them feel that they are part of the brand. This is especially true for brands banking on the human emotional quotient.

Again, pasting a random photo will not do. Always use real situations—something you know your users will do with your product or service. Think about why they would want to visit your site and give them that image in their minds. Flint McGlaughlin from Marketing Experiments says, "A strong face as the primary means of greeting visitors gets a strong reaction that polarizes conversion rates. Never put up a face photo that hasn't been thoroughly tested. It needs to be the right face."

Banking on this statement, think about who your users are, and even if you are using models in your photos make sure they represent your clients. No point putting in a Caucasian face when your target market is an Asian audience.

8. Step-by-Step Images

Step-by-step images work great for instructional blog posts. The PioneerWomanCooks started off as a blog and it's a good example of a blog which featured good quality step-by-step images of recipes. Viewers of her site related to her blog posts because the content was easy to read and fun and the images helped home cooks everywhere understand how their cooking should turn out just by looking at the pictures. Other blogs about recipes also feature images, but it is usually image upon image of the cooked recipe, just from different angles.

If you own and operate an instructional or DIY blog, harness the essence of step-by-step images. Your readers will thank you for it.

Depending on what your product or service is, having quality images is always the right way for marketing. Depending on your budget, you can increase the UX (user experience) by including images on the search results or adding in a 360-degree feature or even a video.

Nobody wants to read a post without images. It is too boring, especially now when readers want information fast. Without images, your posts will encounter less reading. You want more people to read your content and watch your videos. The more they read or watch your content, the more they will like you, and the easier it will be for you to bridge a connection with them. So, always use images in your blog posts.

Conclusion

All the information discussed in this book is really a beginner's guide to understanding the most important facets of an ad campaign on Facebook from creating a campaign, setting up the right creative elements, identifying and targeting your audience, as well as analyzing your campaign's performance.

Despite all this, you must know that advertising, especially the online version, is not a one-size-fits-all kind of marketing. You need to apply what you learn, observe, and test for each ad campaign to the next one so your effort and expenditure pays off. Every business is different. Only you will know the intricacies and nuances of your unique business and how to leverage them with your marketing strategy. Only you will know how your customers respond, and how to apply what you learn effectively.

Facebook Advertising is a must-have marketing tool, especially if you are conducting business online in any capacity. Who knows what other new platforms will exist 5 years from now? Whatever it is, as a marketer, you must take hold of all new and upcoming advertising avenues to reach greater and greater heights in your advertising strategy.